INFORMATION OPERATIONS

Air Force Doctrine Document 3-13
11 January 2005

Incorporating Change 1, 28 July 2011

This document complements related discussion found in Joint Publication 3-13, *Joint Doctrine for Information Operations*.

Cover Sheet for Air Force Doctrine Document (AFDD) 3-13, *Information Operations*

OPR: LeMay Center/DD

28 July 2011

AFDD numbering has changed to correspond with the joint doctrine publication numbering architecture (the AFDD titles remain unchanged until the doctrine is revised). Any AFDD citations within the documents will list the old AFDD numbers until the doctrine is revised. The changed numbers follow:

OLD	NEW	TITLE
AFDD 2-1	changed to AFDD 3-1	*Air Warfare*
AFDD 2-1.1	changed to AFDD 3-01	*Counterair Operations*
AFDD 2-1.2	changed to AFDD 3-70	*Strategic Attack*
AFDD 2-1.3	changed to AFDD 3-03	*Counterland Operations*
AFDD 2-1.4	changed to AFDD 3-04	*Countersea Operations*
AFDD 2-1.6	changed to AFDD 3-50	*Personnel Recovery Operations*
AFDD 2-1.7	changed to AFDD 3-52	*Airspace Control*
AFDD 2-1.8	changed to AFDD 3-40	*Counter-CBRN*
AFDD 2-1.9	changed to AFDD 3-60	*Targeting*
AFDD 2-10	changed to AFDD 3-27	*Homeland Operations*
AFDD 2-12	changed to AFDD 3-72	*Nuclear Operations*
AFDD 2-2	changed to AFDD 3-14	*Space Operations*
AFDD 2-2.1	changed to AFDD 3-14.1	*Counterspace Operations*
AFDD 2-3	changed to AFDD 3-24	*Irregular Warfare*
AFDD 2-3.1	changed to AFDD 3-22	*Foreign Internal Defense*
AFDD 2-4	changed to AFDD 4-0	*Combat Support*
AFDD 2-4.1	changed to AFDD 3-10	*Force Protection*
AFDD 2-4.2	changed to AFDD 4-02	*Health Services*
AFDD 2-4.4	changed to AFDD 4-11	*Bases, Infrastructure, and Facilities* [Rescinded]
AFDD 2-4.5	changed to AFDD 1-04	*Legal Support*
AFDD 2-5	changed to AFDD 3-13	*Information Operations*
AFDD 2-5.1	changed to AFDD 3-13.1	*Electronic Warfare*
AFDD 2-5.3	changed to AFDD 3-61	*Public Affairs Operations*
AFDD 2-6	changed to AFDD 3-17	*Air Mobility Operations*
AFDD 2-7	changed to AFDD 3-05	*Special Operations*
AFDD 2-8	changed to AFDD 6-0	*Command and Control*
AFDD 2-9	changed to AFDD 2-0	*ISR Operations*
AFDD 2-9.1	changed to AFDD 3-59	*Weather Operations*

BY ORDER OF THE
SECRETARY OF THE AIR FORCE

AIR FORCE DOCTRINE DOCUMENT 3-13
11 JANUARY 2005
INCORPORATING CHANGE 1, 28 JULY 2011 |

SUMMARY OF CHANGES

This Interim change to Air Force Doctrine Document (AFDD) 2-5 changes the cover to AFDD 3-13, *Information Operations* to reflect revised AFI 10-1301, Air Force Doctrine (9 August 2010). AFDD numbering has changed to correspond with the joint doctrine publication numbering architecture. AFDD titles and content remain unchanged until updated in the next full revision. A margin bar indicates newly revised material. changes the cover to avoid confusion and a chart has been inserted below outlining new AFDD numbering. A margin bar indicates newly revised material.

Supersedes: AFDD 2-5, 4 January 2002
OPR: LeMay Center/DD
Certified by: LeMay Center/DD (Col Todd C. Westhauser)
Pages: 64
Accessibility: Available on the e-publishing website at www.e-publishing.af.mil for
        downloading
Releasability: There are no releasability restrictions on this publication
Approved by: LeMay Center/CC, Maj Gen Thomas K. Andersen, USAF
        Commander, LeMay Center for Doctrine Development and Education

FOREWORD

Information has long been a key part of human competition—those with a superior ability to gather, understand, control, and use information have always had a substantial advantage on the battlefield. From the earliest recorded battles to the most recent military operations, history is full of examples of how the right information at the right time has influenced military struggles. The Air Force recognizes the importance of gaining a superior information advantage—an advantage obtained through information operations (IO) fully integrated with air and space operations. Today, gaining and maintaining information superiority are critical tasks for commanders and vital elements of fully integrated kinetic and nonkinetic effects-based operations. Information operations are conducted across the range of military operations, from peace to war to reconstitution. To achieve information superiority, our understanding and practice of information operations have undergone a doctrinal evolution that streamlines the focus of IO to improve the focus on warfighting.

The new framework of information operations groups the capabilities of influence operations, electronic warfare operations, and network warfare operations according to effects achieved at the operational level. Each of these capabilities consists of separate and distinct sub-capabilities that, when combined and integrated, can achieve effects greater than any single capability. Integrated Control Enablers (ICE) is a new term used to define what was formerly expressed as information-in-warfare, or IIW. As our understanding of IO has advanced we have come see that ICE are not IO, but rather the "gain and exploit" capabilities that are critical to all air, space, and information operations. This new framework reflects the interactive relationship found between the defend/attack and the gain/exploit capabilities in today's Air Force.

Air Force doctrine recognizes a fully integrated spectrum of military operations. Information operations, like air and space operations, ought to be effects-based. Both air and space operations can support and leverage information operations, just as information operations can support and leverage both air and space operations. Through the horizontal integration of air, space, and IO, we will be able to fully realize the potential of air and space power for the joint force.

Information is both a critical capability and vulnerability across the spectrum of military operations. We are prepared to achieve information superiority across that same spectrum. The United States is not alone in recognizing this need. Potential adversaries worldwide are rapidly improving or pursuing their own information operations capabilities. We will establish information capabilities—and the doctrine to use them—to meet the emerging challenges of the Information Age.

JOHN P. JUMPER
General, USAF
Chief of Staff

TABLE OF CONTENTS

INTRODUCTION

PURPOSE

This Air Force Doctrine Document (AFDD) establishes doctrinal guidance for information operations (IO). More detailed doctrinal discussions of information operations concepts are explained in AFDD 2–5.1, *Electronic Warfare Operations*; AFDD 2–5.2, *Psychological Operations*; and AFDD 2–5.3, *Public Affairs Operations*. The nomenclature of these publications is subject to change. Other AFDDs also discuss information operations as they apply to those specific air and space power functions.

APPLICATION

This AFDD applies to all active duty, Air Force Reserve, Air National Guard, and civilian Air Force personnel.

The doctrine in this document is authoritative, but not directive. Therefore, commanders need to consider the contents of this AFDD and the particular situation when accomplishing their missions. Airmen should read it, discuss it, and practice it.

SCOPE

The Air Force carries out information operations to support national and military objectives. The term "information operations" applies across the range of military operations from peace to war to reconstitution. During crisis or conflict, warfighters conduct information operations against an adversary. However, even when the United States is at peace, the Air Force is fully engaged, conducting IO on a daily basis. For example, because of the increasing dependence on information and the global information environment, the Air Force may be vulnerable to network attack, and so conducts network defense around the clock.

FOUNDATIONAL DOCTRINE STATEMENTS

Foundational doctrine statements are the basic principles and beliefs upon which AFDDs are built. Other information in the AFDDs expands on or supports these statements.

✪ Information operations (IO) are integral to all Air Force operations and may support, or be supported by, air and space operations. (Page 1)

✪ The thorough integration of kinetic and nonkinetic air, space, and information capabilities provides the Air Force with a comprehensive set of tools to meet military threats. (Page 1)

✪ The Air Force defines information superiority as the degree of dominance in the information domain which allows friendly forces the ability to collect, control, exploit, and defend information without effective opposition. (Page 1)

✪ Decision superiority is about improving our capability to observe, orient, decide, and act (OODA loop) faster and more effectively than the adversary. Decision superiority is a relationship between adversary and friendly OODA loop processes. (Page 1)

✪ The three IO capabilities—influence operations, electronic warfare operations, and network warfare operations—while separate and distinct, when linked, can achieve operationally important IO effects. Effective IO depends on current, accurate, and specialized integrated control enablers (ICE) to provide information from all available sources. (Page 4)

✪ Information operations conducted at the operational and tactical levels may be capable of creating effects at the strategic level and may require coordination with other national agencies. (Page 6)

✪ IO should be seamlessly integrated with the normal campaign planning and execution process. There may be campaign plans that rely primarily on the capabilities and effects an IO strategy can provide, but there should not be a separate IO campaign plan. (Page 27)

✪ IO applications span the spectrum of warfare with many of the IO capabilities applied outside of traditional conflict. IO may offer the greatest leverage in peace, pre-conflict, transition-to-conflict, and reconstitution. (Page 27)

✪ Air Force IO may be employed in non-crisis support or military operations other than war (MOOTW) such as humanitarian relief operations (HUMRO), noncombatant evacuation operations (NEO), or counterdrug support missions where Air Force elements are subject to asymmetric threats that could hinder operations or place forces at risk. (Page 27)

✪ IO presents additional challenges in effects-based planning as there are many variables. Many of these variables have human dimensions that are difficult to measure, may not be directly observable, and may also be difficult to acquire feedback. (Page 28)

CHAPTER ONE

THE NATURE OF INFORMATION OPERATIONS

> *Those who are possessed of a definitive body of doctrine and deeply rooted convictions upon it will be in a much better position to deal with the shifts and surprises of daily affairs than those who are merely taking the short views.*
>
> **—Sir Winston Churchill**

GENERAL

Information operations (IO) are the integrated employment of the capabilities of influence operations, electronic warfare operations, and network warfare operations, in concert with specified integrated control enablers, to influence, disrupt, corrupt, or usurp adversarial human and automated decision making while protecting our own. Information operations provide predominantly nonkinetic capabilities to the warfighter. These capabilities can create effects across the entire battlespace and are conducted across the spectrum of conflict from peace to war and back to peace. **Information superiority is a degree of dominance in the information domain which allows friendly forces the ability to collect, control, exploit, and defend information without effective opposition.** Information superiority is a critical part of air and space superiority, which gives the commander freedom from attack, freedom to maneuver, and freedom to attack. **Information operations (IO) are integral to all Air Force operations and may support, or be supported by, air and space operations.** IO, therefore, must be integrated into air and space component operations in the same manner as traditional air and space capabilities **The thorough integration of kinetic and nonkinetic air, space, and information capabilities provides the Air Force with a comprehensive set of tools to meet military threats.**

WARFARE IN THE INFORMATION AGE

Warfare in the information age has placed greater emphasis on influencing political and military leaders, as well as populations, to resolve conflict. Information technology (IT) has increased access to the means to directly influence the populations and its leaders. IT has distributed the process of collection, storage, dissemination, and processing of information. The Air Force goal is to leverage this technology to achieve air, space, and information superiority and to be able to operate in a faster decision cycle (decision superiority) than the adversary. **Decision superiority is a competitive advantage, enabled by an ongoing situational awareness, that allows commanders and their forces to make better-informed decisions and implement them faster than their adversaries can react. Decision superiority is about improving our ability to observe, orient, decide, and act (OODA loop) faster and more effectively than the adversary.** *Joint Vision 2020* describes it as "better decisions arrived at and implemented faster than an opponent can react, or in a non-combat situation, at a tempo that allows the force to shape the situation or react to changes and accomplish its mission." **Decision superiority is a relationship between adversary and friendly OODA loop processes.** Decision superiority is more likely to be achieved if we plan and protect our OODA loop processes in conjunction with analyzing, influencing, and attacking the adversary's. Warfare in the Information Age and its resultant goal of decision superiority have led to a growing reliance on organization and control of information processes, new/enhanced skill sets, rapid development and fielding of new technologies both in existing and new military fields, and their use to confer an operational advantage on commanders of our forces. IT is a dual edged sword. Its use brings risks along with the aforementioned opportunities. The proliferation of IT has provided greater access for individuals to shape perceptions. These means are available to us as well as to our potential adversaries. This convergence of ability to influence populations and our National Military Strategy's growing emphasis on shaping and influencing requires us to reinvigorate the military focus on influence operations. Increasing reliance on networks and the Global Information Grid (GIG), while creating opportunities, also requires better coordination among all users. For example, the trend to take networks mobile requires careful deconfliction in the electromagnetic spectrum for both friendly users and civil users alike. At the same time, we need to remember that the adversary's IO abilities may be unsophisticated, not reliant on modern technology, and yet still be viable and effective. Commanders employing IO must take an integrated effects-based approach to dealing with these realities and provide the framework and process to plan, task, and command and control (C2) these capabilities.

THE INFORMATION ENVIRONMENT

Just a few centuries ago, a commander stood on a hill and observed the battlespace. He used direct observations to orient himself and make decisions via his own cognitive processes, directing his forces through physical means such as hand signals, smoke, drums, flags, voice, or his own actions. Over time new technology and capabilities arose that extended the distance over which a commander controlled forces. Along with greater C2 capabilities, sophisticated intelligence, surveillance, and reconnaissance (ISR) capabilities evolved. This drove the need to develop reports and communications to fuse the sources and translate what others saw into a product to provide the commander situational awareness in order to orient himself to the battlespace and make effective decisions. Eventually, span of control exceeded a single commander's abilities because orientation and decision functions were becoming distributed. Reports and communications became necessary to translate and promulgate commander's intent into action. When IT became available, the need to manage the battlespace's dynamically changing environment quickly drove the development of automated processes of battle management used to synchronize the movements of the military force. Time and experience have taught us the information environment is the aggregate of individuals, organizations, and systems that collect, process, or disseminate information to include the information itself.

This information environment evolved, as shown in figure 1.1, which reconnected the cognitive processes of the decision maker to the physical battle. Realizing the potential, the military quickly started to employ information systems to help with the gathering, manipulation, and dissemination of this information. The growth of IT has connected the greater population to the battlespace, and has increased the importance of information in military operations.

Figure 1.1 illustrates these processes. The green oval (left) depicts the processes used to observe or sense the battlespace. The purple oval (top) depicts the cognitive processes of orienting and deciding on actions to be taken. The yellow oval (right) depicts the process of disseminating intent and orchestrating actions in the environment. These decision processes are not limited to the military; they apply to all organizations and societies. As societies and militaries automate their decision processes, IO presents additional opportunities to have effects in the battlespace such as attacking power grids via a network. Information is itself a weapon and a target.

This model provides a means to understand the IO environment. It also provides a logical foundation for the IO capabilities of influence operations, network warfare operations, and electronic warfare operations. All activities in the physical environment have effects in the cognitive environment. Electronic warfare operates in the electromagnetic spectrum, although it creates effects across the range of the IO operating environment. Network warfare operations are focused on the information domain, which is composed of a dynamic combination of hardware, software, data, and human components. Influence operations are focused on affecting the perceptions and behaviors of leaders, groups, or entire populations. The means of influencing can be physical, informational, or both. The cognitive domain is composed of separate minds and personalities and is influenced by societal norms, thus the cognitive domain is neither homogeneous nor continuous.

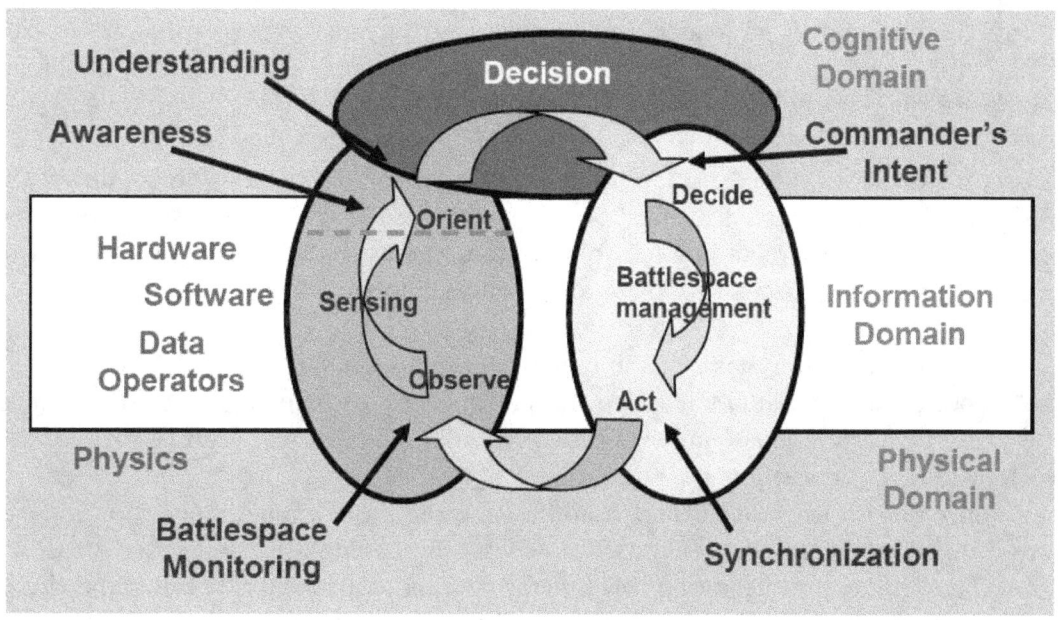

Adapted from *Understanding Information Age Warfare*
David S. Alberts, et al.

Figure 1.1. Information Environment

Societies and militaries are striving to network this "information domain" with the objective of shortening the time it takes for this distributed observe, orient, decide, and act process to occur. It also allows us to automate certain decision processes and to build multiple decision models operating simultaneously. In essence, the information domain continues to expand. New technology increases our society's ability to transfer information as well as an adversary's opportunity to affect that information. Information operations are not focused on making decision loops work; IO focuses on defending our decision loops and influencing or affecting the adversary's decisions loops. **This integration of influence, network warfare, and electronic warfare operations to create effects on OODA loops is the unifying theme of IO.** Whether the target is national leadership, military C2, or an automated industrial process, how the OODA process is implemented provides both opportunities and vulnerabilities.

The potential threats currently facing the United States are no longer defined solely by geographical boundaries or political-military capabilities. Potential adversaries continue to improve their IO capabilities. IO threats can be described as structured or unstructured by looking at their organizational characteristics and purpose. The structured threat is normally well organized, usually having secure financial backing, clear objectives, and the means for infiltrating the information environment. Structured threats include activities by state-sponsored, criminal-sponsored, or ideologically oriented groups with generally long-term objectives. Unstructured threats are generally those threats that originate from individuals or small groups with a limited support structure and limited motives; these threats are not usually sponsored by nation-states or complex organizations. Insiders, those with access to information within an organization, can conduct structured and unstructured threats. Adversaries may recruit some insiders, while other insiders may pursue their own objectives. A wide range of threats exists within the information environment.

As we deal with threats in the information medium, we need to be cognizant that there are basic legal considerations that must be taken into account during all aspects of IO planning and execution, especially regarding network warfare operations. Legal advisors are available at all levels of command to assist with these legal considerations.

Just as the United States plans to employ IO, we should expect our adversaries to do the same. The potential threats and vulnerabilities present additional considerations for commanders. **The three IO capabilities—influence operations, electronic warfare operations, and network warfare operations—while separate and distinct, when linked, can achieve operationally important IO effects. In addition, effective IO depends on current, accurate, and specialized integrated control enablers (ICE) to provide information from all available sources.** The thorough integration of kinetic and nonkinetic air, space, and information capabilities provides the Air Force with a comprehensive set of tools to meet military threats.

Influence Operations

Influence operations are focused on affecting the perceptions and behaviors of leaders, groups, or entire populations. Influence operations employ capabilities to affect behaviors, protect operations, communicate commander's intent, and project accurate information to achieve desired effects across the cognitive domain. These effects should result in differing behavior or a change in the adversary's decision cycle, which aligns with the commander's objectives. **The military capabilities of influence operations are psychological operations (PSYOP), military deception (MILDEC), operations security (OPSEC), counterintelligence (CI) operations, counterpropaganda operations and public affairs (PA) operations.** Public affairs, while a component of influence operations, is predicated on its ability to project truthful information to a variety of audiences.

These activities of influence operations allow the commander to prepare and shape the operational battlespace by conveying selected information and indicators to target audiences, shaping the perceptions of decision-makers, securing critical friendly information, defending against sabotage, protecting against espionage, gathering intelligence, and communicating selected information about military activities to the global audience.

Network Warfare Operations

Network warfare operations are the integrated planning, employment, and assessment of military capabilities to achieve desired effects across the interconnected analog and digital network portion of the battlespace. Network warfare operations are conducted in the information domain through the combination of hardware, software, data, and human interaction. Networks in this context are defined as any collection of systems transmitting information. Examples include, but are not limited to, radio nets, satellite links, tactical digital information links (TADIL), telemetry, digital track files, telecommunications, and wireless communications networks and systems. **The operational activities of network warfare operations are network attack (NetA), network defense (NetD) and network warfare support (NS).**

Electronic Warfare Operations

Electronic warfare operations are the integrated planning, employment, and assessment of military capabilities to achieve desired effects across the electromagnetic domain in support of operational objectives. Electronic warfare operates across the electromagnetic spectrum, including radio, visible, infrared, microwave, directed energy, and all other frequencies. It is responsible for coordination and deconfliction of all friendly uses of the spectrum (air, land, sea, and space) as well as attacking and denying enemy uses. For this reason it is a historically important coordinating element in all operations, especially as current and future friendly uses of the electromagnetic spectrum multiply. **The military capabilities of electronic warfare operations are electronic attack, electronic protection, and electronic warfare support.**

Integrated Control Enablers

Information operations, like air and space operations, are reliant on the integrated control enablers (ICE). ICE includes intelligence, surveillance, and reconnaissance (ISR), network operations (NetOps), predictive battlespace awareness (PBA), and precision navigation and timing (PNT). Information operations are highly dynamic and maneuverable. The transition between the find, fix, track, target, engage, and assess (F2T2EA) phases can be nearly instantaneous. The ICE components support this interactive relationship and strive to provide commanders continuous decision-quality information to successfully employ information operations.

INTEGRATED EFFECTS ACROSS THE BATTLESPACE

Information operations create effects throughout the battlespace during times of peace, pre-conflict, transition-to-conflict, conflict, and reconstitution. IO may not be restricted by either geography or a non-permissive environment. However, some capabilities of IO are bounded by culture, access, technology, or other factors. IO capabilities may be employed at the strategic level while at the same time be employed by military commanders at the operational and tactical levels. The challenge facing commanders is to effectively integrate IO objectives as well as strategic level objectives within the joint force. **Information operations conducted at the operational and tactical levels may be capable of creating effects at the strategic level and may require coordination with other national agencies.**

Influence operations are often designed to affect national leaders, groups, or populations as a whole. Communications networks are often an integral part of national infrastructure and may be vulnerable to attack. The strategic vulnerabilities present in our adversaries may also be present at home. Our strategic defense is highly dependent on IO capabilities. The extent to which IO can contribute to the fight depends on the adversary forces and the level of decision-making superiority attained by friendly forces.

For the commander, Air Force forces/joint force air and space component commander (COMAFFOR/JFACC), IO provides another means to achieve integrated effects across the battlespace (e.g., air superiority, space superiority, and/or information superiority) achieving the joint force commander's (JFC) objectives. This planning effort must take full advantage to integrate IO capabilities with classical or non-IO capabilities to accomplish any and all missions assigned by the JFC. Matching component capabilities to the assigned missions is an essence of operational art.

A necessary first step towards effective air and space component operations is to recognize that air, space, and information operations work best in an integrated and synergistic way. Integrating effects-based information operations with other operations is a crucial part of the Air Force's operational art as it leads to better efficiency and mutual support. It magnifies mass, shapes priority, and can better balance operations across the spectrum. This recognition lays the conceptual foundation for integrating information operations with other air and space operations to achieve air, space, and information superiority. IO is dependent on intelligence, surveillance, and reconnaissance information, intelligence personnel, and an assured combat support infrastructure. The conduct of IO requires unique and detailed intelligence collection agencies and activities. IO combat support requirements must be included in the overall air and space component planning effort. Figure 1.2 depicts this interrelationship.

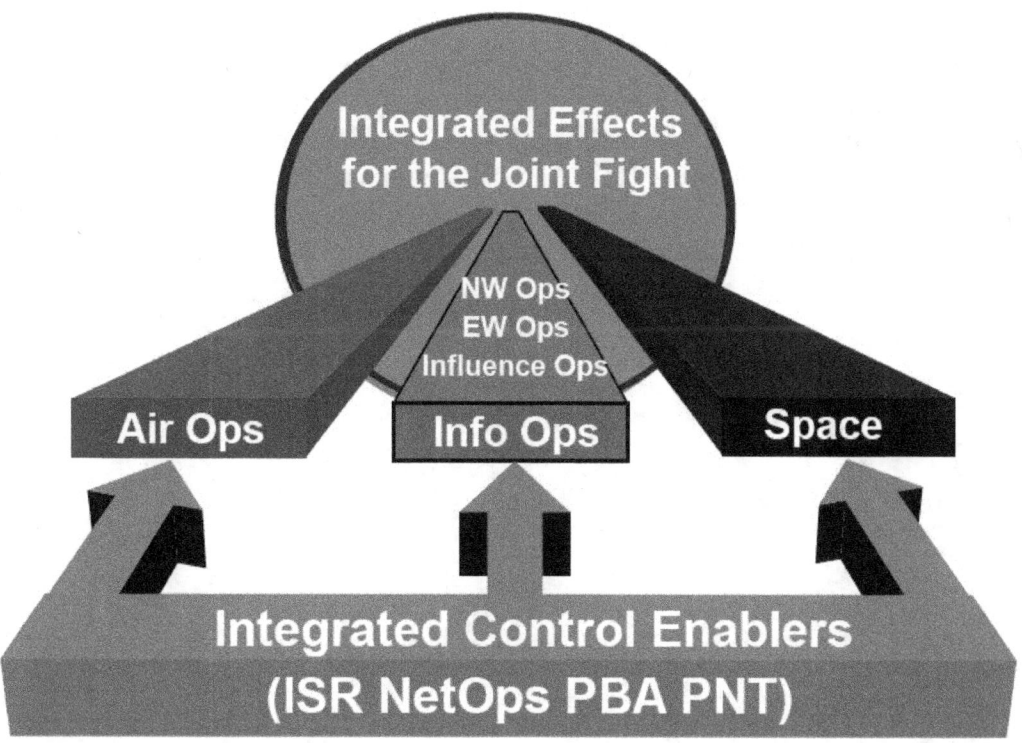

Figure 1.2. Integration of Air, Space, and Information Operations.

Information Superiority

Information superiority is an integral part of air and space superiority, which gives the commander the freedom from attack, the freedom to maneuver, and the freedom to attack. Information superiority is that degree of information advantage of one force over another that permits the conduct of operations at a given time and place without prohibitive opposition. Information operations are not focused exclusively on information superiority and IO alone is not sufficient to achieve information superiority.

Air Superiority

IO is used in achieving air superiority. While EW operations have long been integrated into counterair operations, there are other capabilities of IO that can be used. Network warfare operations can provide spurious, false, and/or misleading information to enemy defensive operations. Influence operations have also been used extensively to achieve air superiority. During Operation DESERT STORM, crews transmitted the term "magnum," as this term indicated the launch of a high-speed antiradiation missile (HARM), to influence adversary surface to air missile (SAM) operators to cease emitting because of the threat of anti-radiation missiles. Planners should take full advantage of IO capabilities when planning and conducting counterair operations.

Space Superiority

Some IO capabilities operate in and through the space environment. Therefore, space superiority is closely related to information superiority. Information superiority can be an enabler for space superiority, and vice-versa. IO can contribute to the effort to deceive, degrade, disrupt, or deny the adversary access to the space environment while protecting our own access. For example, satellite uplinks may be susceptible to jamming or intrusion. An adversary's space-based ISR systems may be vulnerable to jamming, dazzling, or spoofing.

CHAPTER TWO

INFLUENCE OPERATIONS

GENERAL

Influence operations are employment of capabilities to affect behaviors, protect operations, communicate commander's intent, and project accurate information to achieve desired effects across the cognitive domain. These effects should result in differing behavior or a change in the adversary decision cycle, which aligns with the commander's objectives. They should influence adversary decision-making, communicate the military perspective, manage perceptions, and promote behaviors conducive to friendly objectives. Counterpropaganda operations, psychological operations (PSYOP), military deception (MILDEC), operations security (OPSEC), counterintelligence (CI) operations, and public affairs (PA) operations are the military capabilities of influence operations. They support the commander's objectives and support the Air Force in achieving air, space, and information superiority. This is accomplished by conveying selected information and indicators to target audiences; shaping the perceptions of target decision-makers; securing critical friendly information; protecting against espionage, sabotage, and other intelligence gathering activities; and communicating unclassified information about friendly activities to the global audience. These activities of influence operations are often mutually supporting and interrelated. As a result, they must be pre-planned and deconflicted across the spectrum of planning and execution. Integration leads to synergistic effects and effective execution, and helps maintain information consistency. As with all operations, influence operations rely upon accurate and timely intelligence for proper planning, execution, and effects assessment.

The Joint Chiefs of Staff (JCS) Joint Strategic Capabilities Plan (JSCP) recognizes that information is an instrument of national power as important as diplomatic, military, or economic instruments by defining informational flexible deterrent options (IFDOs). IFDOs are included in courses of action (COAs) available to commanders to accomplish operational missions as part of any Flexible Deterrent Option. IFDOs heighten public awareness and promote national and coalition policies, aims, and objectives for the operation, as well as counter adversary propaganda and disinformation in the news.

Credibility is key to influence operations. It is operationally essential that US and friendly forces strive to become the favored source of information—favored because we provide truthful and credible information quickly. It is absolutely imperative that this credibility be established and maintained to ensure confidence in what the US states.

PSYCHOLOGICAL OPERATIONS

Focused on the cognitive domain of the battlespace, PSYOP targets the mind of the adversary. In general, PSYOP seeks to induce, influence, or reinforce the perceptions, attitudes, reasoning, and behavior of foreign leaders, groups, and organizations in a manner favorable to friendly national and military objectives. PSYOP supports these objectives through the calculated use of air, space, and IO with special emphasis on psychological effects-based targeting. Operationally, it provides the COMAFFOR/JFACC an effective and versatile means of exploiting the psychological vulnerabilities of hostile forces to create fear, confusion, and paralysis, thus undermining their morale and fighting spirit.

PSYOP provides key capabilities within the Air Force's IO arsenal. Used in conjunction with other air and space capabilities (e.g., deception, physical attack), it can play a central role in perception management at the strategic, operational, and tactical levels. Ideally, by manipulating, and thus managing, the adversary's perception of the battlespace, the combatant commander can effectively shape, influence, and control the adversary's situational awareness and decision-making process.

Air Force assets have the inherent ability to create psychological effects. For example, satellites and aerial reconnaissance photos can be used to conduct or support PSYOP targeting and discredit adversary claims or intentions. Communications networks, through network warfare operations, can be used to create psychological effects. All aircraft, through visual presence, engine noise, or noise from exploding bombs cause a psychological effect on the adversary by creating fog and friction in the battlespace. Aircraft can also deliver humanitarian aid to maintain support for friendly operations. Additionally, the rapid force projection resulting from the synergistic combination of global air mobility forces and global strike assets empowers the Air Force with the ability to psychologically affect the chosen target population whether it actually inflicts damage or not. Its mere existence is a threat and can be used by influence capabilities to provide a deterrent or behavioral modifier.

PSYOP is also an integral part of joint operations. Air Force PSYOP activities are extensively coordinated throughout the joint force, and in some cases, with the President and/or Secretary of Defense. Thus, the Air Force neither plans nor conducts independent PSYOP campaigns. Rather, Airmen contribute to the theater commander's overall campaign objectives through the systematic use of air and space power, with a view toward shaping the battlespace psychologically. In the larger context of theater influence operations, Air Force PSYOP is designed to complement the methods, practices, and objectives of sister Services, not duplicate them. Air Force PSYOP is also concerned with the development and application of psychologically informed targeting strategies to psychosocially impact adversarial populations.

PSYOP activities can also help defend or safeguard military personnel and resources by preempting the hostile actions of an opposing force or leader, dissuading hostile actors from taking courses of action harmful to the interests or objectives of friendly forces, or countering the effects of hostile propaganda. Thus, PSYOP can be employed across the range of military operations to help counter terrorist threats, protect US forces, dissuade or preempt hostile actors, and support counterpropaganda efforts.

While PSYOP and public affairs operations are separate, distinct activities, they should be coordinated and deconflicted. Public affairs operations disseminate information to national and international audiences, therefore great care must be taken to avoid any public perception that it is slanted or manipulated.

MILITARY DECEPTION

Military deception (MILDEC) capabilities are a powerful tool in military operations and should be considered throughout the operational planning process. Military deception misleads or manages the perception of adversaries, causing them to act in accordance with friendly objectives. Deception planning must begin at the initial stages of operational planning and consider all available military capabilities, therefore the commander's intent is essential to planning and executing MILDEC operations. Subordinate commanders should coordinate with senior commanders to ensure overall unity of effort and deconfliction with the joint deception effort. Additionally, deception operations should be planned from the top down and subordinate deception plans should support higher-level plans.

When formulating the deception concept, particular attention should be placed on defining how commanders would like the adversary to act at critical points. Those desired actions then become the goal of deception operations. Sufficient forces and resources should be committed to the deception effort to make it appear credible to the adversary. Adversary motives and actions must be considered. Accurate and reliable intelligence, surveillance, and reconnaissance operations; information products; and close cooperation with counterintelligence activities help the commander anticipate the adversary's perceptions, intentions, and capabilities.

Deception planning requires the close coordination between operations planners and intelligence specialists to anticipate adversary actions and manipulate adversary perceptions. Intelligence analysts provide intelligence preparation of the battlespace (IPB) products to MILDEC planners to determine the adversary's potential responses to MILDEC operations. Planners conduct COA analysis and/or wargaming to forecast the action, reaction, and counteraction dynamics between friendly and adversary COAs.

A detailed operations security (OPSEC) plan is required and may dictate only a select group of senior commanders and staff officers knows which actions are purely deceptive in nature. Commanders should carefully weigh the balance between OPSEC and detailed coordination of deception plans. In addition, there is a delicate balance between successful deception efforts and media access to ongoing operations. Furthermore, the use of deception in the realm of IO requires particular care and coordination given the speed and potential extent of information propagation. In some cases, excessively restricting the details of planned deception operations can cause confusion at lower echelons that may negatively affect the outcome of the deception operation.

Deception operations span all levels of war and can include, at the same time, both offensive and defensive components. Deception can distract our adversaries' attention from legitimate friendly military operations and can confuse and dissipate adversary forces. However, effective deception efforts require a thorough understanding of an adversary's cultural, political, and doctrinal perceptions and decision-making processes. Planners exploit these factors for successful deception operations. Deception is another force multiplier and can enhance the effects of other air, space, and information operations.

In late 1990, before the start of Operation DESERT STORM, U.S. amphibious training was conducted in the Persian Gulf. The training demonstrated the US forces' amphibious capability, as well as US and Coalition resolve concerning the crisis. Inevitably, journalists asked if an amphibious invasion were planned. In keeping with operational guidelines for discussing information with the media, military officials would not comment on future operations. Even though an amphibious landing ultimately was not conducted during Operation DESERT STORM, Iraqi perception of the US and Coalition capability and resolve may have caused them to conclude that an amphibious invasion was likely. As a result of their perception, Iraqi forces may have focused additional attention and resources that could have been employed elsewhere to defend against an amphibious invasion that never materialized.

Military deception will not intentionally target or mislead the US public, Congress, or the news media. Deception activities potentially visible to the American public should be closely coordinated with PA operations so as to not compromise operational considerations nor diminish the credibility of PA operations in the national media. Public affairs operations should be coordinated and deconflicted with deception planning. Public affairs operations can document displays of force or training operations but they cannot use false information to simulate force projection. Not only is using false information in PA operations contrary to DOD policy and practice, but if false information were ever intentionally used in PA operations, the public trust and support for the Air Force could be undermined and PA operations would be degraded.

OPERATIONS SECURITY

Operations security (OPSEC) is an activity that helps prevent our adversaries from gaining and exploiting critical information. OPSEC is not a collection of specific rules and instructions that can be applied to every operation, it is a methodology that can be applied to any operation or activity for the purpose of denying critical information to the adversary. Critical information consists of information and indicators that are sensitive, but unclassified. OPSEC aims to identify any unclassified activity or information that, when analyzed with other activities and information, can reveal protected and important friendly operations, information, or activities. A critical information list should be developed and continuously updated in peacetime as well as during a contingency. The critical information list helps ensure military personnel and media are aware of non-releasable information.

OPSEC should be coordinated with all the activities of information operations. Controlling the adversary's access to information by denying or permitting access to specific information can shape adversaries perceptions. An OPSEC vulnerability may be desired to achieve a PSYOP or deception objective.

> *Unclassified information and indicators may provide our adversaries with important information about friendly operations. Pre-crisis deployments for stage operations and/or force projection signal US intentions due to diplomatic clearance requirements, to include overflight, landing, and beddown of forces and airfield assessment teams. Time-phased force deployment data and force deployment plans are vulnerable to exploitation as are commercial carriers augmenting mobility deployments.*

Air Force commanders at all levels ensure OPSEC awareness and that appropriate OPSEC measures are implemented continuously during peacetime and times of conflict. Commanders should provide OPSEC planning guidance to the staff at the start of the planning process when stating the "commander's intent" and subsequently to the supporting commanders in the chain of command. By maintaining a liaison with the supporting commanders and coordinating OPSEC planning guidance, commanders can help ensure unity of effort in gaining and maintaining the essential security awareness considered necessary for success.

COUNTERINTELLIGENCE

The Air Force Office of Special Investigations (AFOSI) initiates, conducts, and/or oversees all Air Force counterintelligence (CI) investigations, activities, operations, collections, and other related CI capabilities. **Counterintelligence is defined as information gathered and activities conducted to protect against espionage, other intelligence activities, sabotage, or assassinations conducted by or on behalf of foreign governments or elements thereof, foreign organizations, or foreign persons, or international terrorist activities.** AFOSI supports influence operations through CI operations designed to detect, destroy, neutralize, exploit, or prevent espionage activities through identification, manipulation, deception, or repression of the adversary. Counterintelligence operations are performed at all levels and support national, joint, and Air Force commander objectives. Counterintelligence capabilities should be fully integrated into all planning and execution efforts.

Counterintelligence support to influence operations includes the identification of threats through CI collections and analysis, and assessment of threats through reactive and proactive means. Documentation of the threat through ISR processes and counterintelligence products are the primary methods of notification of the threat to commanders. Neutralization and exploitation of threats through investigation and operations are also a counterintelligence capability.

Successful CI and OPSEC deny adversaries useful information on friendly forces, and CI operations may support PSYOP and MILDEC objectives through proper integration into planning. Finally, counterintelligence personnel should be included as part of the Information Warfare Flight (IWF) and liaise closely with the air and space operations center (AOC). CI inclusion in planning and operations is a necessary capability in development of full spectrum IO capabilities to meet the combatant commander's objectives.

PUBLIC AFFAIRS OPERATIONS

Commanders conduct PA operations to assess the information environment in areas such as public opinion and to recognize political, social, and cultural shifts. Public affairs operations are a key component of informational flexible deterrent options and build commanders' predictive awareness of the international public information environment and the means to use information to take offensive and preemptive defensive actions in Air Force operations. Public affairs operations are the lead activity and the first line of defense against adversary propaganda and disinformation. Falsehoods are easily identified when the truth is well known.

By disseminating timely, accurate information about air and space capabilities, preparations, and results, PA operations enhance Air Force morale and readiness to accomplish the mission, gain and maintain public support for military operations, and communicate US resolve in a manner that provides global influence and deterrence. These capabilities are delivered through four core tasks: media operations, internal information, community relations, and strategic communication planning. (Refer to the AFDD on public affairs for a detailed discussion)

Commanders face the challenge of balancing the task of informing the public with the need to maintain operations security, a traditional cornerstone of successful military planning and execution. Communicating Air Force capabilities can be a force multiplier and may deter potential adversaries by "driving a crisis back to peace" before use of force becomes necessary.

Maintaining an open dialogue with internal and external news media communicates the leadership's concern with the issues and allows accurate information to be provided to Air Force and public sector audiences. Providing the information quickly and accurately establishes credibility with media representatives and the public, helping to ensure the Air Force gains and maintains the information initiative. Providing public information heightens public awareness and helps gain and maintain public support. Increased media attention and public debate may also place enormous pressures on foreign leaders and governments and that alone may be enough to achieve the commander's objective.

While the release of sensitive or critical information may be perceived as detrimental to military operations, commanders should consider the possible advantages of releasing certain information to demonstrate US resolve, intent, or preparations. Rather than providing an advantage to an adversary, the carefully coordinated release of operational information in some situations could deter military conflict. Making international audiences aware of forces being positioned overseas and US resolve to employ those assets can enhance support from friendly countries. The same information may also deter potential adversaries. If adversaries aren't deterred from conflict, information revealing US or friendly force capabilities and resolve may still affect adversary decision-makers. Public affairs operations should be coordinated and deconflicted with other activities of influence operations because communication technology can make information simultaneously available to domestic and international audiences. Public affairs operations must never be used to mislead the public, national leaders, or the media.

Commanders should integrate public affairs operators into information operations planning and execution to gain synergistic effects that enhance the ability to achieve military objectives. Coordination and deconfliction with public affairs operations help to ensure the credibility of US operations and communications is retained. Otherwise, public trust and support for the Air Force could be undermined or lost. (See the AFDD on Public Affairs Operations for an expanded discussion of public affairs operations)

COUNTERPROPAGANDA OPERATIONS

The Air Force defines counterpropaganda operations as activities to identify and counter adversary propaganda and expose adversary attempts to influence friendly populations and military forces situational understanding. They involve those efforts to negate, neutralize, diminish the effects of, or gain an advantage from foreign psychological operations or propaganda efforts. Numerous organizations and capabilities (e.g., ISR activities, public affairs, or other military units and commanders) can identify adversarial propaganda operations attempting to influence friendly populations and military forces. Commanders at all levels should integrate activities designed to disseminate truthful information; mitigate adversary messages; and disrupt, degrade, and disable adversary psychological operations. Such efforts might range from specific public affairs operations to convey accurate information to the targeted audiences and mitigate the intended effects of an adversary's psychological operations, to efforts to physically destroy adversary PSYOP resources and assets.

Public affairs operations are often the lead activity in counterpropaganda operations. Gaining and maintaining the information initiative in a conflict can be a powerful weapon to defeat propaganda. The first out with information often sets the context and frames the public debate. It is extremely important to get complete, truthful information out first—especially information about friendly forces' mistakes, so that it is friendly forces that expose the errors and put them into accurate context. This helps to disarm the adversary's propaganda and defeat attempts by the adversary to exploit these mistakes for their propaganda value.

Adversaries of the United States have used propaganda during many conflicts and most propaganda activities play out through the domestic and international news media. While we may anticipate propaganda being used against the United States, PA operations will not willingly or intentionally misinform the US public, Congress, or US media.

SUPPORTING ACTIVITIES

Influence operations are most successful through the seamless integration of kinetic and nonkinetic capabilities. Influence operations may be supported and enhanced by physical attack to create or alter adversary perceptions. Influence operations require support from many Air Force capabilities to include tailored ISR, combat camera operations, and cultural expertise.

Physical attack disrupts, damages, or destroys adversary targets through destructive power. Physical attack can also be used to create or alter adversary perceptions. In either case, the purpose of physical attack in supporting information operations affects adversary information or information systems by using a physical weapon to create a specific effect on the adversary.

For example, well-timed physical attacks can add credibility to and intensify a previously delivered PSYOP message. Physical attack can also be used to drive an adversary to use certain exploitable information systems. Kinetic and nonkinetic attack operations should be integrated in the targeting process. Information operations should be carefully coordinated and deconflicted with other planning efforts to include physical attack.

Because all military operations strive to produce some level of influence on adversaries or allies, influence operations, as an information operation, should not be confused with kinetic capabilities that may have influential effects. For example, a B-52 dropping Mk-82s near an enemy division could conduct air operations to support an influence objective. This is not IO, but should be integrated and closely coordinated with IO capabilities. Influence operations effects should result in differing behavior or a change in the adversary decision cycle, which aligns with the commander's objectives.

Among the many challenges combatant commanders face to influence enemy decision-makers and combatants, they also have to win over either a hostile or neutral general population or keep from alienating the friendly population. Humanitarian efforts from food and supplies distribution to public health and emergency medical support can and do make a difference. These operations can support influence operations, and should be incorporated into IO planning.

Intelligence, surveillance, and reconnaissance are fundamental to successful influence operations. Some examples include: analyzing target audiences and adversary decision-makers, identifying opportunities for influence, and analyzing sources of access. Although all source intelligence is fundamental to successful IO, human intelligence, requested and tasked through the joint collection function, can provide a significant amount of validity to the application of information and intelligence to a target population because of its cultural and language background.

Air Force combat camera can provide support to influence operations. Some examples are on-demand images and multimedia services. Photographic activities cover the full spectrum of air and space functions, notably aerial documentation and editing of weapon system video-- the gun camera footage. OPSEC should be considered prior to public release of combat camera products.

CULTURE AND WORLDVIEW

Actions and words have different effects on different cultures. What we perceive is not necessarily what another culture may perceive. Worldview is described as a shared sense of reality by a group of people and is formed by values, preferences, beliefs, experiences, expectations, and language. Knowledge of other cultures enhances our effectiveness and helps to ensure our activities do not create misunderstandings or unintended negative attitudes. There are resources, in addition to academic works, that can provide insight into different cultures.

Foreign Area Officers (FAOs) have expertise in the military, economy, culture, history, government, and language of their target region or countries within their region. Political-military (Pol-Mil) affairs officers plan, formulate, coordinate, and help implement international politico-military policies for specific regions or countries. Both FAO and Pol-Mil expertise can provide insight into the perceptions and mindsets of the foreign audience. Additionally, religion is an aspect of culture. Religion is both a component of worldview and a source of information. The Chaplain's office can provide insight into the religious aspects of a culture's worldview. Finally, culture is fundamentally about human behavior and group dynamics. The Surgeon General's office is uniquely qualified to advise on individual and group behavior. The ability to convey the intended message and achieve the desired effects is predicated upon understanding the values, history, motivation, behavior, attributes, and perceptions of target cultures.

CHAPTER THREE

NETWORK WARFARE OPERATIONS

> *We need to be able to think in terms of target effects. I picture myself around that same targeting table where you have the fighter pilot, the bomber pilot, the special operations people and the information warriors. As you go down the target list, each one takes a turn raising his or her hand saying, "I can take that target."*
>
> —General John P. Jumper
> Commander, U.S. Air Forces in Europe
> Defense Colloquium on Information Operations, March 25, 1999

GENERAL

Network warfare operations (NW Ops) are conducted throughout the spectrum of conflict on a continual basis and must be integrated with other air and space operations. NW Ops, like all other IO, are most effective and efficient when integrated with other air and space operations. NW Ops are the integrated planning, employment, and assessment of military capabilities to achieve desired effects across the interconnected analog and digital network portion of the battlespace. NW Ops are conducted through a dynamic combination of hardware, software, data, and human components in the information domain. Information, information systems and networks, and the Global Information Grid (GIG) exist in the information domain. Examples include, but are not limited to, radio nets, satellite links, tactical digital information links (TADIL), telemetry, digital track files, telecommunications, and wireless communications networks and systems. The transmission can be analog or digital and can be bounded (e.g., coaxial cable) or unbounded (e.g., free space). Networks in this context are defined as an interconnected and interrelated collection of systems storing or transmitting information.

Maintaining or gaining technological advantage in relation to our adversaries is a challenging goal. The information domain encompasses several media, and rapid advances in technology make technological superiority fleeting. A perceived advantage in information technology (IT) can also be turned into a disadvantage. New technologies introduce new vulnerabilities for exploitation through manipulation or attack. The approach to NW Ops must remain flexible in order to adapt as technology advances.

NETWORK WARFARE OPERATIONS

Network warfare operations (NW Ops) are the integration of the military capabilities of network attack (NetA), network defense (NetD), and network warfare support (NS). The integrated planning and employment of network warfare operations along with electronic warfare operations (EW Ops), influence operations, and other military capabilities are conducted to achieve desired effects across the information domain. Network warfare operations, when employed with other information operations, ensure our forces operate in a protected information environment, allowing air and space operations to be conducted in an unfettered fashion. NW Ops can also be used independently or in conjunction with other operations to create effects in the adversary's battlespace.

Network Attack

Network attack (NetA) is employment of network-based capabilities to destroy, disrupt, corrupt, or usurp information resident in or transiting through networks. Networks include telephony and data services networks. Additionally, NetA can be used to deny, delay, or degrade information resident in networks, processes dependent on those networks, or the networks themselves. A primary effect is to influence the adversary commander's decisions. NetA can contribute effects in support of all air and space power functions. One example of NetA includes actions taken to reduce an adversary's effectiveness by denying the adversary use of their networks by affecting the ability of the network to perform its designated mission. NetA may support deception operations against an adversary by deleting or distorting information stored on, processed by, or transmitted by network devices. Psychological operations can be performed using NetA to target and disseminate selected information to target audiences. NetA can also offer the commander the ability to incapacitate an adversary while reducing exposure of friendly forces, reducing collateral damage, and saving conventional sorties for other targets. Network attack, like all other information operations, is most effective and efficient when combined with other air and space operations. Certain aspects of electronic warfare operations overlap NetA and should be coordinated. An example of this is where concurrent physical attack integrated with NetA can protect our operations and technology, while exploiting adversarial vulnerabilities.

Military forces under a combatant commander derive authority to conduct NetA from the laws contained in Title 10 of the U.S. Code (U.S.C.). However, the skills and target knowledge for effective NetA are best developed and honed during peacetime intelligence or network warfare support (NS) operations. Intelligence forces in the national intelligence community derive authority to conduct network exploitation and many NS operations from laws contained in U.S.C. Title 50. For this reason, "dual-purpose" military forces are funded and controlled by organizations that derive authority under laws contained in both Title 10 and Title 50. The greatest benefit of these "dual-purpose" forces is their authority to operate under laws contained in Title 50, and so produce actionable intelligence products, while exercising the skills needed for NetA. These forces are the preferred means by which the Air Force can organize, train, and equip mission-ready NetA forces.

Network Defense

Network defense (NetD) is employment of network-based capabilities to defend friendly information resident in or transiting through networks against adversary efforts to destroy, disrupt, corrupt, or usurp it. NetD can be viewed as planning, directing, and executing actions to prevent unauthorized activity in defense of Air Force information systems and networks and for planning, directing, and executing responses to recover from unauthorized activity should it occur. Commanders should provide NetD planning guidance to the staff, as well as to subordinate and supporting commanders, as part of the "commander's intent." NetD actions include analyzing network activity to determine the appropriate course of action (COA) to protect, detect, and react to internal and external threats to Air Force networks. Determining the nature of the threat to friendly systems often requires the fusion of ISR, counterintelligence, blue force vulnerability, and operational considerations. This analytical effort leads to the development of appropriate defensive COAs to the unauthorized activity. In a notional example, distributed electronic sensors and/or human operators would serve as the "trip wire" initially to indicate an Air Force network is under attack. Next, analysis of the attack fused with operational considerations would further define the nature of the threat to Air Force systems. This analysis then assists in the development of a comprehensive range of COAs to respond to the attack. Commanders select the most appropriate COAs and execute those actions to defend networks. Additional post-event protection measures may be implemented to counter the specific tactics and techniques used during the attack. Our doctrine anticipates the need for an active defense in response to unauthorized activities.

NetD includes strategic global network operations, theater or regional operations, and local garrison or deployed base operations. Each operation falls within the command authority of the JFC and supporting Air Force component commanders assigned the functional NetD mission for that AOR.

Network Warfare Support

Network warfare support (NS) is the collection and production of network related data for immediate decisions involving NW Ops. NS is critical to NetA and NetD actions to find, fix, track, and assess both adversaries and friendly sources of access and vulnerability for the purpose of immediate defense, threat prediction and recognition, targeting, access and technique development, planning, and execution in NW Ops. NS spans the range of operations from peace to war and back to peace. While NW Ops requires support from all intelligence sources, NS requires particularly close coordination with SIGINT collection, processing, exploitation, and dissemination. Due to the focus of NS, gain and exploit activities deal with technical data that is unique and requires analysts with specialized skills. Significant expertise covering a range of skills includes, but is not limited to, scientists, signals analysts, computer programmers, computer technicians, and operators. Typically these skill are found in "dual-purpose" forces operating under authority of laws contained in U.S.C Title 50, and as such can ensure resources are available to collect, analyze, and disseminate products to support NW Ops requirements.

Products resulting from this collection and exploitation process include the network order of battle and parametric data reflecting the characteristics of various network threat and target systems. NS data are used to produce intelligence, or provide targeting and engagement data for electronic, network, or influence attack. Specifically, NS provides profiling, event analysis, open source review, as well as pattern analysis in support of NetD and countermeasure development. Likewise, NS provides nodal and system analysis and engineering to identify potential vulnerabilities in adversary systems to support NetA. Additionally, NS performs full spectrum and cryptological planning and deconfliction.

PRESENTATION OF NETWORK WARFARE OPERATIONS FORCES

The character of NW Ops allows for multiple planning and execution options to meet a theater JFC's objectives. NW Ops may be planned and conducted across the information domain from locations outside the JFC's theater of operations.

Presenting NW Ops forces that do not move forward as a force package requires special considerations in the force planning process. Careful consideration must be given to establishing C2 relationships, planning activities to synchronize COA options and execution, and force sustainment.

The COMAFFOR, through his or her A-6 directorate, has operational responsibility for delivering, monitoring, protecting, and managing networks within an area of responsibility (AOR). Networks in this context are defined as a collection of systems transmitting and receiving information including radio nets, satellite links, tactical digital information links (TADIL), telemetry, digital track files, telecommunications, and wireless communications networks and systems. This system of systems creates a network-centric environment that is commanded and controlled at the Air Force level by the AFNetOps/CC. The AFNetOps/CC supports the A-6, who coordinates with the supporting theater C4 control center (TCCC), theater NetOps center (TNC), Service network operations and security center (NOSC), AOC communications focal point, and AOC IO team to formulate COAs for the COMAFFOR and C/JFACC to consider for countering emerging enterprise threats.

NW Ops are often conducted by dual-purpose or high-demand/low-density forces. NetA also has unique requirements such as planning and force generation, which involve engineering development, integration, and regression testing. NW Ops require a unique presentation of forces to the theater.

The supported COMAFFOR leverages the AFFOR rear to apply Air Force skills, intelligence, and capabilities to the fight. Under direction of the COMAFFOR, the AFFOR rear staff draws on Air Force experts to perform intelligence, COA development, and engineering assessments in support of the supported COMAFFOR's objectives. Once a COA is selected, the reachback support staff generates a tailored attack force that may execute under the TACON of the supported commander best able to synchronize the NetA with the supported operation. This same AFFOR rear structure is used to support planning and generate tailored forces for NS operations. Many times IO can have the greatest effect before the initiation of hostilities. In order to leverage some of these capabilities the COMAFFOR must sometimes rely upon organizations that are able to operate under the authority of laws contained in U.S.C. Title 50. Close attention to the command relationships is necessary in all situations of NetA and NS in order to comply with US policy, and laws.

CHAPTER FOUR

ELECTRONIC WARFARE OPERATIONS

GENERAL

Electronic warfare (EW) is any military action involving the use of electromagnetic or directed energy to manipulate the electromagnetic spectrum or to attack an adversary. **The Air Force describes electronic warfare operations (EW Ops) as the integrated planning, employment, and assessment of military capabilities to achieve desired effects across the electromagnetic domain in support of operational objectives.** The EW spectrum is not merely limited to radio frequencies but also includes optical and infrared regions as well. EW assists air and space forces to gain access and operate without prohibitive interference from adversary systems, and actively destroys, degrades, or denies opponents' capabilities, which would otherwise grant them operational benefits from the use of the electromagnetic spectrum. During Operation DESERT STORM, effective force packaging, which included self-protection, standoff, and escort jamming and anti-radiation attacks, contributed significantly to the air components' success and survivability. In Operation ALLIED FORCE (OAF), multi-service capabilities were combined in the form of "jam to exploit," demonstrating how opponent communications users can be herded to frequencies which intelligence may collect and exploit. In Operation IRAQI FREEDOM (OIF), EW planning via an EW Coordination Cell (EWCC) extended and enhanced EW planning and execution capabilities, and coordination with the AOC staff. EW has demonstrated it provides commanders valuable effects across the battlespace.

ELECTRONIC WARFARE OPERATIONS

EW is a key contributor to air superiority, space superiority, and information superiority. The most important aspect of the relationship of EW to air, space, and information operations is that EW enhances and supports all operations throughout the full spectrum of conflict. Air Force EW resources and assets may take on new roles in support of operations as the electronic warfare operation mission evolves.

The three military capabilities of EW operations are electronic attack (EA), electronic protection (EP), and electronic warfare support (ES). All three contribute to air and space operations, including the integrated IO effort. Control of the electromagnetic spectrum is gained by protecting friendly systems and countering adversary systems.

Electronic attack (EA) is the division involving the use of electromagnetic, directed energy (DE), or anti-radiation weapons to attack personnel, facilities, or equipment with the intent of deceiving, disrupting, denying, and/or destroying adversary combat capability. It also deceives and disrupts the enemy integrated air defense system (IADS) and communications, as well as enables the destruction of these adversary capabilities via lethal strike assets. Successful EA against serious threats frequently involves employing combinations of EA capabilities based on the known or suspected disposition and performance characteristics of adversary threat systems in ways which allows a COMAFFOR/JFACC to achieve desired effects with acceptable risk. Suppression of enemy air defenses (SEAD) is the cross-doctrinal construct that integrates EW, as an element of IO, with physical attack capabilities such as the use of high-speed anti-radiation missiles (HARMs) against enemy IADS. (See the AFDDs in the Air Warfare series of publications for an expanded discussion of physical attack.)

Electronic protection (EP) enhances the use of the electronic spectrum for friendly forces. Electronic protection is primarily the defensive aspect of EW that is focused on protecting personnel, facilities, and equipment from any effects of friendly or adversary employment of electronic warfare that degrade, neutralize, or destroy friendly combat capability.

Electronic warfare support (ES), the collection of electromagnetic data for immediate tactical applications (e.g., threat avoidance, route selection, targeting, or homing) provides information required for timely decisions involving electronic warfare operations. This intimate relationship with SIGINT collection, processing, exploitation, and dissemination spans the range of operations from peace to war and back to peace, and employs significant expertise covering a range of skills including scientists, signals analysts, computer programmers, and EW technicians and operators. Products resulting from this collection and exploitation process include an electronic order of battle (EOB) and parametric data reflecting the electronic characteristics of various EW threat systems, which aid detection and countermeasure employment. The intelligence community provides support in this area.

EW serves many missions in different ways. For example, combat missions typically focused on dealing with sophisticated IADS employ EW as an integral part of their SEAD operations. Missions that require undetected ingress and egress from airspace consciously reject physical attack as detrimental to their primary mission objectives and rely on EW to assist in deception. The mobility air forces (MAF) generally accept aircraft arrivals and departures to be in the "public domain" and are more concerned with infrared (IR) man portable air defense systems (MANPADS) and effective countermeasures than with radio frequency detection and tracking in the vicinity of airfields. Space operators are concerned about adversarial jamming of communication uplinks or downlinks as well as jamming or disrupting space-based ISR systems, or other forms of communications denial or deception. To adequately address this full range of interests, EW requires an extensive system of SIGINT collection, processing, evaluation, and dissemination dedicated to the identification and characterization of systems operating in the electromagnetic spectrum. The intelligence community also provides support in this area.

Because of the extensive range of operations supported by EW, it is important to distinguish the roles of electromagnetic spectrum users. Spectrum users fall into several categories based on their objectives. There are a few users whose functions may fall exclusively in the spectrum. Jamming and SIGINT collection are examples. The majority of users, however, use electronic equipment as one of many means of accomplishing their missions. EW does not claim ownership of these electronic systems, but serves to coordinate and deconflict the many uses of the spectrum by all the users.

The warfighting aspect of EW occurs only in the context of an adversarial force that gains operational benefit from their use of the electromagnetic spectrum. EW is the process of retaining the advantages of spectrum use for friendly forces while consciously denying, degrading, disrupting, deceiving, and/or destroying adversarial spectrum capabilities and requires a well developed and executed EW plan.

EW is a force multiplier. Control of the electromagnetic spectrum can have a major impact on success across the range of military operations. Proper employment of EW enhances the ability of operational commanders to achieve objectives. Electronic attack, electronic protect, and electronic warfare support must be carefully integrated to be effective. The commander should ensure maximum coordination and deconfliction between EW, ISR gain and exploit operations, strategic plans, current operations, current plans, NW Ops, and influence operations. When EW actions are fully integrated with military operations and the above operations, synergy is achieved, operational advantage is gained and maintained, attrition is minimized, and effectiveness is enhanced.

A joint EW Coordination Cell (EWCC) may be established to centralize EW planning and coordination efforts. This type of cell was successfully employed in OIF. This reflected a progression of more formal and effective EW planning and execution from operations in the Balkans to Iraq. The EWCC is an organizational entity established to coordinate, deconflict, and provide EW operational direction for friendly users of the electromagnetic spectrum versus adversarial uses of the spectrum. In addition to accomplishing coordination and planning with other EW functions, the EWCC should also coordinate with other IO functions through appropriate elements of the IWF.

CHAPTER FIVE

INFORMATION OPERATIONS PLANNING AND EXECUTION

GENERAL

Information operations are integral to military operations and are a prerequisite for information superiority. IO supports, and may also be supported by, air and space operations and needs to be planned and executed just like air operations. **IO should be seamlessly integrated with the normal campaign planning and execution process. There may be campaign plans that rely primarily on the capabilities and effects an IO strategy can provide, but there should not be a separate IO campaign plan.** IO applications span the range of military operations with many of the IO capabilities applied outside of traditional conflict. Figure 5.1 provides some examples of the application of IO throughout the range of military operations. The role of IO in peace, pre-conflict, transition to conflict, and reconstitution may offer the greatest leverage. **Air Force IO may be employed in non-crisis support or military operations other than war (MOOTW) such as humanitarian relief operations (HUMRO), noncombatant evacuation operations (NEO), or counterdrug support missions where Air Force elements are subject to asymmetric threats that could hinder operations or place forces at risk.** During conflict, the balanced application of kinetic and nonkinetic capabilities achieves the greatest synergistic effects at the strategic, operational, and tactical levels.

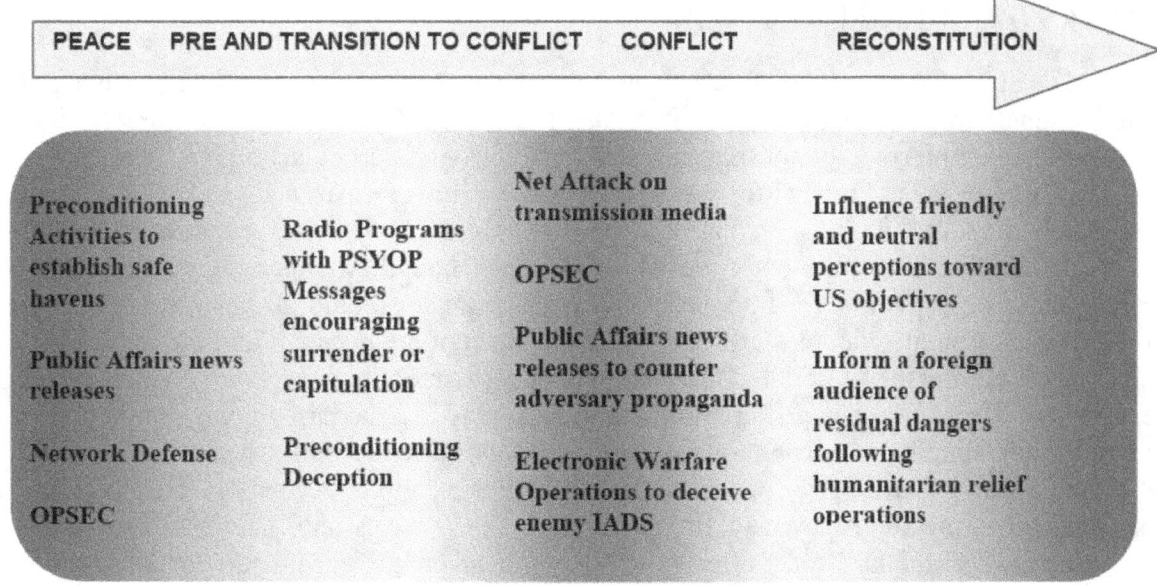

Figure 5.1. Information Operations Throughout the Range of Military Operations

> **Combat Search and Rescue (CSAR) Operations**
>
> *Information operations are capable of creating effects throughout the battlespace and from peace to war. CSAR operations often begin prior to the initiation of combat operations. IO capabilities can be used to create safe areas in an area sympathetic to the US or friendly cause. Rewards can be offered for aiding friendly forces. During execution, IO can help protect isolated personnel by denying information to enemy forces looking for the individuals. OPSEC and deception are always a consideration when planning and executing CSAR operations.*

INFORMATION SUPERIORITY

One of the commander's priorities is to achieve decision superiority over an adversary by gaining information superiority and controlling the information environment. This goal does not in any way diminish the commander's need to achieve air and space superiority but rather facilitates efforts in those areas and vice versa. The aim of information superiority is to have greater situational awareness and control than the adversary. Effective use of IO leads to information superiority. The effort to achieve information superiority depends upon two fundamental components: an effects-based approach, and well-integrated IO planning and execution accomplished by IO organizations. The following paragraphs discuss these important components.

EFFECTS-BASED APPROACH

The ability to create the effects necessary to achieve campaign objectives, whether at the strategic, operational, or tactical levels, is fundamental to the success of the Air Force. An effect is the anticipated outcome or consequence that results from a particular military operation. The emphasis on effects is as crucial for successful IO as for any other air and space power function. Commanders should clearly articulate the objectives or goals of a given military operation. Effects should then flow from objectives as a product of the military operations designed to help achieve those objectives. Based on clear objectives, planners should design specific operations to achieve a desired outcome, and then identify the optimum capability for achieving that outcome. It is important to realize that operational assessment may be more challenging in IO because the effects are often difficult to measure. IO may also be based upon common sense, a rule of thumb, simplification, or an educated guess that reduces or limits the search for solutions in domains that are difficult or poorly understood. For example, psychological effects are not only difficult to measure; they may also not manifest themselves until later in time. There are also second-order and third-order effects that should be taken into consideration, and again, these may not manifest themselves until much later. **IO presents additional challenges in effects-based planning as there are many variables. Many of these variables also have human dimensions that are difficult to measure, may not be directly observable, and may also be difficult to acquire feedback.** At all times, objectives must be set and effects must be analyzed from the point of view of the culture where operations are being conducted. Assessment is inherently more challenging and is predisposed to a lesser degree of accuracy than conventional battle damage assessment (BDA). Nevertheless, the planning of IO should be focused on operational objectives and the effects produced. Critical to the effects-based approach is the requirement to be able to measure, to the greatest extent possible, IO effects. Operational assessment allows the commander to evaluate IO and adjust specific information operations to evolving combat situations to increase its effectiveness. The following sections provide examples of the types of effects IO can achieve and provide a brief review of the targeting process.

Aerial pictures help the military assess bomb damage to a target. The softer kind of strike is harder to assess. Information warfare experts look for what they call, "The voilà moment." In Afghanistan, a lesson learned was the importance in explaining, "Why are we here?" The majority of Afghanis did not know that September 11 occurred. They didn't even know of our great tragedy. The voilà moment came when the population understood why coalition forces were fighting the Taliban and Al Qaeda.

Firing Leaflets and Electrons
New York Times
February 23, 2003

Strategic Effects

Strategic effects can be created by a wide variety of military actions occurring at all levels of war. Information operations are capable of creating effects at the strategic level and require coordination with other instruments of national power. In addition, planners and operators need to know that tactical level IO events have the potential to create strategic effects. Influence operations are often designed to affect national leaders or their population as a whole. Communications networks are often an integral part of national (strategic) infrastructure and may be vulnerable to attack. Those strategic vulnerabilities present in our adversaries may also be present at home and, as a result, our strategic defense is highly dependent on the IO capabilities that create information, air, and space superiority.

Information operations at the strategic level of war are directed by the President or Secretary of Defense and planned in coordination with other agencies or organizations outside the Department of Defense (DOD). Such operations should be coordinated among supporting Air Force units, the combatant commander's IO team or cell, and other supporting components, as applicable, to ensure unity of effort and prevent conflict with possible ongoing operational-level efforts. However, due to the sensitivity of such operations, they may not always be coordinated with other units, but rather synchronized and deconflicted at higher levels. Operations should be synchronized and deconflicted at the lowest level possible to accommodate these sensitivities.

Specific strategic effects IO can achieve at this level are to:

✪ Influence both friendly and adversarial behavior conducive toward achieving national objectives through the promotion of durable relationships and partnerships with friendly nations.

✪ Institute appropriate protective and defensive measures to ensure friendly forces can continuously conduct IO across the entire spectrum of conflict. Such measures create effects that deny adversaries knowledge of, or the ability to access or disrupt, friendly information operations.

✪ Reduce adversary leadership resistance to US national objectives by affecting willpower, resolve, or confidence.

✪ Create a lack of confidence in an adversary's military, diplomatic, or economic ability to achieve its goals or defeat US goals.

✪ Negatively impact an adversary's ability to lead by affecting their communications with their forces or their understanding of the operating environment.

✪ Deter aggression, support counterproliferation of weapons of mass destruction, support homeland defense, and support counterterrorism.

✪ Employ actions that reduce friendly vulnerabilities to physical and cyber attacks.

Operational Effects

Operational effects can be created by a wide variety of military actions occurring at all levels of war. IO at the operational level of war can be conducted by the COMAFFOR within the assigned area of responsibility or joint operation area at home or abroad. IO at this level involves the use of military assets and capabilities to achieve operational effects through the design, organization, integration, and conduct of campaigns and major operations. The COMAFFOR should retain command and control of IO assets where the preponderance of effects supports the COMAFFOR's assigned missions. IO plans between and among supported and supporting commands should be coordinated closely to prevent redundancy, mission degradation, or fratricide. Specific effects IO can achieve at this level include:

✪ Hindering an adversary's ability to strike by incapacitating their information-intensive systems and creating confusion in the operational environment.

✪ Slowing or ceasing an adversary's operational tempo by causing hesitation, confusion, and misdirection.

✪ Reducing an adversary's command and control capability while easing the task of the war-to-peace transition.

✪ Using information operations techniques instead of physical destruction, preserving the physical integrity of some targets for later use, both by friendly forces and the local populace, which can reduce or prevent reconstruction costs during the war-to-peace transition.

✪ Influencing adversary and neutral perceptions of leaders, military forces, and populations, away from adversary objectives and toward US objectives.

- Enhancing US plans and operations by disrupting adversary plans.

- Negatively impacting an adversary's ability to lead by affecting their communications with their forces or their understanding of the operating environment.

- Disrupting the adversary commander's ability to focus combat power.

- Influencing the adversary commander's estimate of the situation. By creating confusion and inaccuracy in the assumptions an adversary makes about the situation, the direction and outcome of adversary military operations can be shaped.

- Employing actions that reduce friendly vulnerabilities to physical and cyber attacks.

- Protecting forces during HUMRO and NEO operations from asymmetric threats

Tactical Effects

Tactical effects can be created by a wide variety of military actions. The COMAFFOR or functional component commander directs the execution of tactical-level IO. The primary focus of IO at the tactical level of war is to deny, degrade, deceive, disrupt, or destroy an adversary's use of information and information systems relating to C2, intelligence, and other critical information-based processes directly related to conducting military operations. Specific effects may be to:

- Deny, degrade, disrupt, deceive, or destroy adversary capabilities and information on friendly forces.

- Reduce the capability of adversary forces. Destroy an adversary's capability to communicate.

- Influence adversary perception of friendly forces, operations, and capabilities.

- Protect friendly information and information systems to give friendly forces the ability to leverage information to accomplish the mission.

- Maintain the element of surprise by denying the adversary warning on friendly force movements.

Targeting

The purpose of targeting is to achieve specific desired effects at the strategic, operational, and tactical levels of war. A target is a specific area, object, audience, function, or facility subject to military action on which we want to create an effect. Targeting is a comprehensive and involved process of matching a target within the cognitive, information, or physical domain with kinetic weapons or nonkinetic capabilities. Targeting involves recommending to the commander those targets that when attacked may help achieve his objectives and the best weapons (lethal and nonlethal, kinetic or nonkinetic) to achieve a desired effect. The targeting process cuts across organizational and traditional functional boundaries. Reachback, liaison, and coordination with other organizations possessing nonkinetic capabilities and specific IO expertise, is essential. Functional areas such as air operations, intelligence, space operations, logistics, and communications must be closely integrated throughout the targeting process. Close coordination, cooperation, and communication among the participants are essential.

> *Information operations played a key role enabling the collapse of the Iraqi command and control structure and the rapid success of the coalition campaign in Operation IRAQI FREEDOM (OIF). The combined forces air and space component commander (CFACC) embedded IO experts within each planning cell throughout the AOC. In addition to regular integration of information with other operations, they tracked, prioritized, and apportioned nonkinetic effects with traditional kinetic operations. Finally, these individuals often synchronized IO effects to prepare the battlespace for kinetic operations. When the Iraqi integrated air defense system had to be dismantled to protect coalition air operations, a range of options from bombing facilities to psychological operations and disrupting communications links was available. Using information operations in combination with kinetic operations collapsed the Iraqi command and control structure, neutralized the Iraqi integrated air defense system while reducing the destruction to facilities and reducing the number of sorties and risk to pilots flying over Iraq.*

Clear objectives and commander's guidance are the foundation of the targeting process. Quantifiable and clear objectives and guidance are best for effective operations. Objectives are developed at the national, theater, and component levels. The commander's guidance is normally provided at the national, theater, and component levels. IO targeting nominations originate from IO subject matter experts integrated into the AOC and JTF targeting processes for approval, coordination, and deconfliction. IO planners should use established targeting processes and methodologies to recommend targets in which IO can be used to support the theater campaign plan.

INFORMATION OPERATIONS ORGANIZATIONS

A number of Air Force organizations contribute to effective IO. The following discuss several of the key organizations employed in information operations.

Information Warfare Flight (IWF)

IO can be conducted throughout the spectrum of peace and conflict. In peacetime, the major command/numbered air force (MAJCOM/NAF) IWF is the operational planning element for IO and may coordinate IO actions when an air and space operations center (AOC) has not been activated. When the AOC is activated, a portion of the IWF is established as an IO team and integrates into the warfighting divisions within the AOC (Strategy, Plans, ISR, Combat Operations, etc.). The IO team provides the IO expertise to plan, employ, and assess IO capabilities prior to the initiation of hostilities, transition to conflict, and reconstitution. It is important to note that some information operations are planned and/or executed throughout the Air Force every day, regardless of the status of an operational AOC. Examples may include

OPSEC, network exploitation, NetD and public affairs. These operations may support objectives beyond the purview of a single combatant commander. For these reasons, the IWF acts as the unifying element for information operations conducted across the spectrum of peace and conflict.

During peacetime, the IWF coordinates (when tasked) with Service, joint, and national-level organizations to plan and achieve effects which will deter, or if deterrence fails, influence, shape, and prepare the battlespace for effective follow-on air, space, and information operations. To ensure the proper expertise is maintained, IWFs also train and exercise their readiness to support the AOC's wartime missions. In addition, the IWFs develop and review the IO portion of operational plans and use existing intelligence analysis to support peacetime operations through transition to conflict while maintaining close working relationships with external IO-related activities. Successful military operations must carefully integrate both offensive and defensive IO capabilities. An integrated approach, combining all the tools, disciplines, and capabilities of electronic warfare operations, network warfare operations, and influence operations will yield the best long-term effects. Commanders use their operational judgment to determine the best approach and should ensure their staffs carefully consider both the advantages and disadvantages of specific IO capabilities in their scheme of maneuver.

During the transition to conflict, reconstitution phases of a campaign plan, and upon activation of the AOC, the IWF becomes the Air Force's key IO expertise normally presented through the AOC. The AOC typically is the main organizational structure through which the capabilities of EW Ops, NW Ops, and influence operations planning and execution are integrated and synchronized. Based on the commander's direction and guidance, the IWF's IO team may also design and execute portions of the campaign that rely on IO capabilities to accomplish the commander's objectives. The IO team's primary focus is to plan and integrate IO capabilities into the commander's air and space operations, and is closely associated with Special Technical Operations (STO).

IO planning, execution, coordination, targeting, monitoring, adjustment, and assessment are integrated by the IWF's IO team members within the AOC. During OIF, these IO team members were embedded into the strategy, combat plans, air mobility, combat operations, and ISR divisions, to develop IO rules of engagement (ROE), and fuse target nominations into attack plans, tasking orders, and special instructions (SPINS). The IO team should ensure the ROEs and IO operating requirements and authorizations are taken into consideration. The IO team should coordinate IO-specific intelligence requests and requirements with the ISR division. When necessary, the team should be in contact with liaisons of the appropriate assets to resolve problems and coordinate requirements and taskings. The merger of the IO team's disciplines into the AOC promotes timely integration of kinetic and nonkinetic force options into the deliberate air tasking order (ATO) planning and execution process. If a combatant commander is supported by or supports a functional combatant commander who has execution authority over Air Force IO, they may have more options to meet the JFC objectives with coordination through their respective AOCs.

For contingency operations not requiring combat air forces (CAF) participation, the AOC may consist of an air mobility division (AMD) or a special operations liaison element (SOLE). The IWFs are structured differently to support their respective global and unique mission areas.

Again, IO has a role in all operations, from peace to war to reconstruction, and should be integrated in the planning and execution of all missions or operations.

There are basic legal considerations that must be taken into account during all aspects of IO planning and execution, especially with regards to NetA. Legal advisors are available at all levels of command in order to assist with these legal considerations. Examples of such considerations may include a transition from defensive to offensive actions, ROE, and the Law of Armed Conflict, as well as the applicability of treaties and agreements.

IO requires coordination among all in-theater operations, including organizations providing reachback support. When the JFACC is not an Air Force officer, the COMAFFOR still ensures coordination among IO actions both internally and externally with other joint force IO organizations. IO capabilities should be considered as an integral part of the Air Force, and integrated into the overall theater campaign, and not just as an add-on.

The normal coordination and integration process within a joint task force is highlighted below:

- The JFC develops theater campaign objectives and normally designates a joint force IO officer to accomplish broad IO oversight functions. The joint force IO officer heads the JFC IO team, when designated.

- The JFC IO team (composed of select representatives from each staff element, Service component, and supporting agencies responsible for integrating the capabilities and disciplines of IO) develops IO options in support of JFC objectives. These options may be broad or specific, but should not direct the details of execution. Detailed execution is left to the components to accomplish. This process adheres to the Air Force tenet of centralized control and decentralized execution. This means that the component commander should set the priority, effects, and timing for all IO operations.

- Service components address component objectives and the desired effects required to achieve them. Primary and supporting components are designated by the JFC.

- The AOC IO team takes air component tasks, as determined by the JFC's objectives, the component objectives, and the commander's intent for planning and integration. The IO team helps integrate IO capabilities into the joint air and space operations plan (JAOP) and ATO.

- The AOC IO team members should meet regularly with the IWF to develop, coordinate and deconflict IO into the warfighting COAs. The IO team should seamlessly integrate the planning results through the AOC divisions into the JAOP, and the ATO/tasking process for commander's approval. The JFC IO team or cell may also serve to coordinate or deconflict Service component operations COAs if required.

- The COMAFFOR should retain command and control of IO assets where the preponderance of effects supports the COMAFFOR's assigned missions.

34

The IO team should ensure the rules of engagement and IO operating requirements and authorizations, such as special target lists, are taken into consideration. The team should coordinate and follow up upon IO-specific intelligence requests and requirements through the ISR division and stay in contact with the appropriate assets to resolve problems and coordinate requirements and taskings. Likewise, the team chief should help ensure target deconfliction.

EW Ops Organizations

Electronic warfare is conducted by units with capabilities ranging across the electronic attack, protect, and support functions. EW operations require attention before, during, and after military operations. A joint EW coordination cell (EWCC) is the necessary planning and execution organization to orchestrate the activities of units to achieve EW objectives of the campaign plan.

During peacetime, designated EW personnel are tasked to review combatant commander plans to prepare for EW operations. These reviews consist of at least four elements. First is familiarization and critical assessment of the standard uses of the electromagnetic spectrum by military, civil, commercial, maritime, and other users in the region. Second is familiarization with the forces apportioned to the combatant commander for the approved course of action (COA). Third is review and assessment of signals intelligence (SIGINT) sources and dissemination applicable to the plan. The fourth element is the review resulting in the initial planning for execution of the campaign's EW thread. Planning should include definition of the size and support for the required EWCC, delegation of necessary joint EW coordination authorities among Services based on the preponderance of military assets being provided, and relations within and outside the AOC.

When military activities appear likely and crisis action planning commences, the COMAFFOR's EWCC should be established to directly plan and coordinate with the JFC and component staffs to insure integration of EW in the overall campaign plan. It is also effective to conduct planning conferences with participating MAJCOMs, other Services and coalition partners, as well as members of the IWF, to bring the collaborative EW effort into focus.

As military actions become imminent and the formal staffs of the JFC and JFACC are activated, the EWCC structure, led by the appropriate Service and augmented by other Service and coalition partners, will coordinate and synchronize all component EW Ops activities. In cases where the Air Force is the designated lead Service, the EWCC will be a distinct organization in the AOC. EWCC will take advantage of technical and professional expertise located outside the AOR via reachback to provide detailed analysis of the adversary EOB, influence force apportionment, component coordination, and development and execution of EW Ops procedures consistent with the coordinated campaign EW thread.

When military activities decline and eventually cease, the EWCC will prepare for post-engagement activities by coordinating follow-on collection and dissemination activities with the ISR division, information operations, and other members of the staff, and coordinate redeployment actions.

Network Defense and Network Operations Organizations

NetD and NetOps organizations provide the JFC with critical capabilities to realize the effects of information and decision superiority.

Collectively, these organizations provide varying degrees of NetD and NetOps support. They provide commanders with real-time intrusion detection and perimeter defense capabilities, network management and fault resolution activities, data fusion, assessment, and decisions support.

During employment, the organizations are arranged into a three-tiered operational hierarchy, which facilitates synchronized application of their collective capabilities in support of the DOD's defense-in-depth security strategy.

In-Garrison Tier 1 Organizations

Tier 1 organizations are considered operational level entities and are at the top of the three-tiered hierarchy. As such, they are responsible for planning, coordinating, tasking, and directing the overall Service-wide NetOps and NetD efforts. They provide global-level NetOps and NetD C2 of in-garrison Air Force networks and serve as the Air Force NetD component to US Strategic Command. Consisting of a C2 operations center, staff, and on-alert crews, this organization executes authority to task operational and tactical-level entities (tier 2 and tier 3) in response to events that cross multiple tier 2 boundaries, affect the preponderance of the Air Force network, or are time critical to assure network availability and security. An example today is the Air Force network operations security center (AFNOSC).

In-Garrison and Deployed Tier 2 Organizations

As the middle entity, tier 2 organizations are hybrid in nature and provide commanders with a set of operational and tactical capabilities. In their tactical role they are responsible for employing their capabilities in support of the operational tasking assigned by tier 1 organizations supporting the JFC. However, in their operational capacity, tier 2 organizations are responsible for exercising C2 over all tier 3 entities within their assigned area of operations.

Organizational capabilities include, but are not limited to, providing commanders near-real time situational awareness of networks within their area of operations, and the ability to develop and execute effective countermeasures in response to friendly and adversary events that threaten network availability and security. An example of this garrison organization today is the network operations security center (NOSC). A deployed example is referred to as a NOSC-D.

In-Garrison and Deployed Tier 3 Organizations

Tier 3 organizations are at the bottom of the hierarchy and are purely tactical level entities. However, depending on the source of threat, they are considered the first and last line of defense in executing the DOD's defense-in-depth strategy. In addition to employing capabilities to support tier 1 and 2 objectives, tier 3 organizations are responsible for providing the wing and theater air base commanders with the means to achieve information and decision superiority in support of higher level operational and strategic objectives. An example of this garrison organization today is the network control center (NCC) and its deployed equivalent is the NCC-D.

Other Reachback Support

Commanders and their staffs should consider all the resources and capabilities available through reachback methods. There are many Service, joint, DOD, and national agencies and organizations listed earlier in this publication that can provide additional support to theater IO efforts. The AOC combat plans and ISR divisions should be the main forward organizations requesting additional support.

CHAPTER SIX

INTEGRATED CONTROL ENABLERS

> *Before the bombs started dropping on downtown Baghdad, we were preparing the battlespace in southern Iraq.*
>
> **—Major General Paul J. Lebras**
> **Commander, Air Intelligence Agency**

GENERAL

Information operations, like all Air Force operations, depend on a seamless continuum of gain, exploit, disseminate, decide, attack, and defend. The integrated control enablers (ICE) include gain, exploit, and disseminate capabilities that continuously provide commanders decision quality information, and also include the commander's ability to monitor, command, control, and defend forces and assets assigned.

INTEGRATED CONTROL ENABLERS

Information operations are dependent on ICE. **The integrated control enablers are critical capabilities required to execute successful air, space, and information operations and produce integrated effects for the joint fight. These include intelligence, surveillance, and reconnaissance (ISR), network operations (NetOps), predictive battlespace awareness (PBA), and precision navigation and timing (PNT).** Information operations are highly dynamic and maneuverable. The transition between the find, fix, track, target, engage, and assess (F2T2EA) phases can be nearly instantaneous. The ICE components support this interactive relationship and strive to provide commanders continuous decision-quality information to successfully employ information operations capabilities.

Network Operations and Information Assurance

NetOps encompasses information assurance (IA), system and network management, and information dissemination management. The Air Force and joint community have come to recognize these pillars as information assurance and network defense, enterprise service management/network management, and content staging/information dissemination management respectively. NetOps consists of organizations, procedures, and functionalities required to plan, administer, and monitor Air Force networks in support of operations and also to respond to threats, outages, and other operational impacts. NetOps includes the continuous oversight and management of Air Force-wide networks. The Air Force established a commander of Air Force NetOps (AFNetOps/CC) as well as the Air Force Network Operations and Security Center (AFNOSC) to conduct this function. NetOps also includes theater or regional network command and control with MAJCOMs providing administrative control (ADCON) functions supporting their respective combatant commanders and tactical control (TACON) by tasked COMAFFORs and their respective joint force commanders. The overarching mission of NetOps is to ensure air, space, and IO are unimpeded by friendly or adversary activities on the net. NS and NetD are focused exclusively on finding, fixing, tracking, targeting, engaging, and assessing adversaries to assure information on the network is defended. NetOps are the integrated planning and employment of military capabilities to provide the information assurance for the friendly net environment needed to plan, control, and execute military operations and conduct Service functions.

Information assurance (IA) comprises those measures taken to protect and defend information and information systems by ensuring their availability, integrity, authenticity, confidentiality, and non-repudiation (ability to prove sender's identity and prove delivery to recipient). IA spans the full lifecycle of information and information systems. IA depends on the continuous integration of trained personnel, operational and technical capabilities, and necessary policies and procedures to guarantee continuous and dependable information, while providing the means to efficiently reconstitute these vital services following disruptions of any kind, whether from an attack, natural disaster, equipment failure, or operator error. In an assured information environment, warfighters can leverage the power of the information age.

Developing and implementing security and protection in the 21st century require recognition of the globalization of information and information systems. The Air Force employs a defense-in-depth philosophy by providing layered and integrated protection of information, information systems, and networks. The defense-in-depth approach employs and integrates the abilities of people, operations, and technology to establish multilayer, multidimensional protection. Security and protection include the policies and programs to help counter internal and external threats—whether foreign or domestic—to include protection against trusted insider misconduct or error. Security, like interoperability, must be incorporated into information systems designs from the beginning to be effective and affordable. Level of protection must be commensurate to the importance and vulnerability of the specific information and information systems.

Traditional programs such as communications security (COMSEC) and emissions security, as well as NetD, are methods to protect our information and information systems. In addition, other information assurance programs help assess the interoperability, compatibility, and supportability of our information systems and aim specifically to reduce vulnerabilities and to improve the overall security of networks and systems shared by all.

Due to the US dependency on and the general vulnerability of information and its supporting systems, NetOps and IA are essential to IO.

Intelligence, Surveillance, and Reconnaissance

ISR is the integrated capabilities to task, collect, process, exploit, and disseminate accurate and timely intelligence information. ISR is a critical function that helps provide the commander the situational and battlespace awareness necessary to successfully plan and conduct operations. Commanders use the intelligence information derived from ISR assets to maximize their own forces' effectiveness by optimizing friendly force strengths, exploiting adversary weaknesses, and countering adversary strengths. This resource pool includes Air Force, joint, and national agency assets (e.g., NSA, DIA, CIA, NRO, NGA, DHS, DISA). To be fully effective, the ISR process must be integrated into the full range of command and control processes and operations. All operations, including IO, depend on effective ISR. Effective IO actions require current, accurate, and specialized ISR information from all available sources.

Predictive Battlespace Awareness

Effective IO depends upon a successful PBA. As a maturing concept, PBA is "knowledge of the operational environment that allows the commander and staff to correctly anticipate future conditions, assess changing conditions, establish priorities, and exploit emerging opportunities while mitigating the impact of unexpected adversary actions" (Air Force Pamphlet 14-118). In order to accomplish this, PBA lays out a methodology that enables integration of all intelligence, surveillance, and reconnaissance assets available to commanders, in order to maximize their ability to predict enemy courses of action and decide friendly courses of action. One of the first steps in PBA is assessing friendly vulnerabilities and adversary strengths and weaknesses in order to predict enemy courses of action through IPB. This level of awareness requires development and integration of five key activities: IPB, target development, ISR strategy and planning, ISR employment, and assessment. These activities are continuously refined in parallel to provide a seamless understanding of the battlespace.

Precision Navigation and Timing

Synchronization and integration of military capabilities have always been critical in battle, but never more important than in today's modern combat. Precision navigation and timing (PNT) provided by space-based systems are essential to IO by providing the ability to integrate and coordinate IO force application to create effects across the battlespace.

CHAPTER SEVEN

EDUCATION AND TRAINING

> *I'm firmly convinced that leaders are not born; they're educated, trained, and made, as in every other profession. To ensure a strong, ready Air Force, we must always remain dedicated to this process.*
>
> **—General Curtis E. LeMay**
> **CSAF, 1961-1965**

Education and training provide the foundation for conducting effective information operations. All Airmen should have a general understanding of information operations capabilities. As in other specialties, IO personnel should be thoroughly trained in the specific IO processes that relate to their particular field of expertise. IO personnel should recognize the contribution their functional specialty makes to the warfighter to help achieve the goal of information superiority. The intent of IO education and training is to ensure Air Force IO operators clearly understand the principles, concepts, and characteristics of information operations. Finally, while not every Airman needs a comprehensive course in information operations, every Airman should understand that IO is a key function of the Air Force distinctive capabilities of information superiority and air and space superiority.

TRAINING, EXERCISES, WARGAMES AND EXPERIMENTS

IO encompasses many Air Force specialties performing widely varying functions. Therefore, individual training progression is best left to specialty experts. As Air Force operators, IO professionals need to receive specialty training within their assigned duties, then initial IO qualification training followed by mission qualification training at the unit level. Other training programs, such as continuation training, exist to help experienced specialists plan and execute integrated information operations.

Realistic IO training provided through exercises is essential to proficiency and readiness. Exercises train individuals, units, and staffs in the necessary skills and tools for IO and ensure that staffs can plan, control, and support such operations. Planners should create and integrate realistic and challenging field training exercises, modeling and simulations, seminars, and command post exercises that allow commanders, staffs, and units to participate in information operations. Additionally, wargaming systems and simulators should be capable of simulating IO capabilities and their effects on target systems. Exercises should emphasize employment operations, as well as deployment and redeployment phases, and the transition to and from war. Commanders at all levels should participate in exercises to familiarize themselves with the complexities and details of IO doctrine and operations. This participation would build confidence in employment of IO as a warfighting capability. Exercises, wargames and experiments are essential for highlighting possible shortfalls and corrective actions to achieve success in future operations. Commanders should seek the participation of other Services, US national agencies as well as foreign military Services to improve interoperability in these training exercises. Commanders should also continually assess the impact of IO training, exercises, and ongoing peacetime missions on their units' ability to conduct wartime missions.

IO must be integrated into Air Force education, training, and exercise programs as the means to bring IO into Air Force culture and combat capability. Experiments and wargames contribute to the advancement of IO by exploring new processes and technologies to improve IO as a whole. IO provides capabilities that can be employed in peacetime as well as contingency and combat operations. To support presentation of forces to joint warfighters, Air Force education, training, exercises, and experiments must emphasize the integration, synchronization, and deconfliction of IO in all AOC processes. This includes strategy and plans development, tasking, execution monitoring and control, and assessment.

At the very Heart of Warfare lies doctrine …

SUGGESTED READINGS

Air Force Publications (Note: All Air Force doctrine documents are available on the Air Force Doctrine Center web page at https://www.doctrine.af.mil)

Air Force Doctrine Document 1, *Air Force Basic Doctrine*

Air Force Doctrine Document 2, *Organization and Employment of Aerospace Power*

Air Force Doctrine Document 2-5.2, *Psychological Operations*

Air Force Doctrine Document 2-5.3, *Public Affairs Operations*

Air Force Doctrine Document 2-8, *Command and Control*

Air Force Pamphlet 14-118, *Aerospace Intelligence Preparation of the Battlespace*

Joint Publications

Joint Publication 0-2, *Unified Action Armed Forces (UNAAF)*

Joint Publication 3-13, *Joint Doctrine for Information Operations*

Joint Publication 3-53, *Doctrine for Joint Psychological Operations*

Joint Publication 3-54, *Joint Doctrine for Operations Security*

Joint Publication 3-58, *Joint Doctrine for Deception Operations*

Other Publications

Presidential Decision Directive 63, *Critical Infrastructure Protection.* 22 May 1998.

Presidential Decision Directive 68, *International Public Information.* 30 April 1999.

Other Suggested Readings

Alberts, David, Garstka, John, and Frederick Stein. *Network-Centric Warfare: Developing and Leveraging Information Superiority.* 2nd Revised Edition. (Washington DC: National Defense University Press). 2000.

Alberts, David; Garstka, John; Hays, Richard; and David Signori. *Understanding Information Age Warfare.* (Washington DC: National Defense University Press). 2001.

Arquilla, John and David Ronfeldt. *Swarming & The Future of Conflict.* (Santa Monica, Rand). 2000.

Arquilla, John and David Ronfeldt. *In Athena's Camp: Preparing for Conflict in the Information Age.* (Rand Corporation). 1997.

Baier, Frederick L., Capt, USAF. *50 Questions Every Airman Can Answer.* (Maxwell AFB, AL: Air University Press). 1999.

Campen, Alan D. *The First Information War: The Story of Computers and Intelligence Systems in the Persian Gulf War.* (AFCEA International Press). 1992.

Daniel, Donald C., and Katherine L. Herbig. "Propositions on Military Deception," *Military Deception and Strategic Surprise*, pp. 154-177. Edited by John Gooch and Amos Perlmutter. (London: Frank Cass & Co.). 1982.

Denning, Dorothy. *Information Warfare and Security.* (Addison Wesley Longman, Inc.). 1998.

Goldstein, Frank L., Col, USAF ed. *Psychological Operations: Principles and Case Studies.* (Maxwell AFB, AL: Air University Press). 1996.

Hall, Wayne. *Stray Voltage: War in the Information Age.* (Annapolis, MD: Naval Institute Press). 2003.

Khalilzad, Zalmay and John White. *The Strategic Appraisal: The Changing Role of Information in Warfare.* (Rand Corporation). 1999.

Rattray, Gregory. *Strategic Warfare in Cyberspace.* (Cambridge, MA: The MIT Press). 2001.

Roszak, Theodore. *The Cult of Information: A Neo-Luddite Treatise on High-Tech, Artificial Intelligence, and the True Art of Thinking.* 2nd ed. (Berkley and Los Angeles, CA: University of California Press). 1994.

Schleher, D. Curtis, Dr. *Introduction to Electronic Warfare.* (Dedham, MA: Artech House). 1986.

Stein, George, Dr. "Information Warfare: Words Matter." *InfoWar*, pp.51-59. Edited by G. Stocker and C. Schöpf. (New York & Vienna: Springer). 1998.

Taylor, Philip M. *Munitions of the Mind: A History of Propaganda from the Ancient World to the Present Day.* (New York: Manchester University Press). 1995.

Tsoukas, H. "The Tyranny of Light," *Futures.* (November 1997).

GLOSSARY

Abbreviations and Acronyms

ACO	airspace control order
ADCON	administrative control
AFCERT	Air Force computer emergency response team
AFDD	Air Force doctrine document
AFFOR	Air Force forces
AFNOSC	Air Force network operations security center
AFOSI	Air Force Office of Special Investigations
AFSC	Air Force specialty code
AOC	air and space operations center
ATO	air tasking order
BDA	battle damage assessment
C2	command and control
CAF	combat air forces
CERT	computer emergency response team
CI	counterintelligence
CIA	Central Intelligence Agency
COA	course of action
COMAFFOR	commander, Air Force forces
COMSEC	communications security
DHS	Department of Homeland Security
DIA	Defense Intelligence Agency
DISA	Defense Information Systems Agency
DOD	Department of Defense
EA	electronic attack
EBO	effects-based operations
EOB	electronic order of battle
EP	electronic protection
ES	electronic warfare support
EWCC	electronic warfare coordination cell
EW Ops	electronic warfare operations
F2T2EA	find, fix, track, target, engage, assess
GIG	Global Information Grid
HUMRO	humanitarian relief operation

IA	information assurance
IADS	integrated air defense system
ICE	integrated control enablers
IFDO	informational flexible deterrent options
IO	information operations
IPB	intelligence preparation of the battlefield
IR	infrared
ISR	intelligence, surveillance, and reconnaissance
IT	information technology
IW	information warfare
IWF	information warfare flight
JCS	Joint Chiefs of Staff
JFACC	joint force air component commander [JP 1-02] joint force air and space component commander {USAF}
JFC	joint force commander
JP	joint publication
MAAP	master air attack plan
MAF	mobility air forces
MAJCOM	major command
MANPAD	man portable air defense system
MD	military deception
MOE	measures of effectiveness
MOOTW	military operations other than war
NCC	network control center
NCC-D	network control center -- deployed
NetA	network attack
NetD	network defense
NEO	noncombatant evacuation operation
NetOps	network operations
NGA	National Geospatial-Intelligence Agency
NOSC	network operations and security center
NOSC-D	network operations and security center (deployable)
NRO	National Reconnaissance Office
NS	network warfare support
NSA	National Security Agency
NW Ops	network warfare operations
OODA	observe, orient, decide, act
OPCON	operational control
OPSEC	operations security
PA	public affairs

PBA	predictive battlespace awareness
PNT	precision navigation and timing
PSYOP	psychological operations
ROE	rules of engagement
SEAD	suppression of enemy air defenses
SIGINT	signals intelligence
STO	special technical operations
TACON	tactical control
TADIL	tactical digital information link
TTP	tactics, techniques, and procedures

Definitions

battlespace. The environment, factors, and conditions which must be understood to successfully apply combat power, protect the force, or complete the mission. This includes the air, land, sea, space, and the included enemy and friendly forces, facilities, weather, terrain, the electromagnetic spectrum, and information environment within the operational areas and areas of interest. (JP 1-02) [*The commander's conceptual view of the area and factors which he must understand to successfully apply combat power, protect the force, and complete the mission. It encompasses all applicable aspects of air, sea, space, and land operations that the commander must consider in planning and executing military operations. The battlespace dimensions can change over time as the mission expands or contracts, according to operational objectives and force composition. Battlespace provides the commander a mental forum for analyzing and selecting courses of action for employing military forces in relationship to time, tempo, and depth.*] [AFDD 1] {Words in brackets apply only to the Air Force and are offered for clarity.}

command and control. The exercise of authority and direction by a properly designated commander over assigned and attached forces in the accomplishment of the mission. Command and control functions are performed through an arrangement of personnel, equipment, communications, facilities, and procedures employed by a commander in planning, directing, coordinating, and controlling forces and operations in the accomplishment of the mission. Also called **C2**. (JP 1-02)

counterintelligence. Information gathered and activities conducted to protect against espionage, other intelligence activities, sabotage, or assassinations conducted by or on behalf of foreign governments or elements thereof, foreign organizations, or foreign persons, or international terrorist activities. Also called **CI**. (JP 1-02)

counterpropaganda operations. Those psychological operations activities that identify adversary propaganda, contribute to situational awareness, and serve to expose adversary attempts to influence friendly populations and military forces. (JP 1-02) [*Activities to identify and counter adversary propaganda and expose adversary attempts to influence friendly* *populations and military forces situational understanding.]* (AFDD 2-5) {Words in brackets apply only to the Air Force and are offered for clarity.}

deception. Those measures designed to mislead the enemy by manipulation, distortion, or falsification of evidence to induce the enemy to react in a manner prejudicial to the enemy's interests. (JP 1-02)

decision superiority. A competitive advantage, enabled by an ongoing situational awareness, that allows commanders and their forces to make better-informed decisions and implement them faster than their adversaries can react. (AFDD 2-5)

electronic warfare. Any military action involving the use of electromagnetic and directed energy to control the electromagnetic spectrum or to attack the enemy. Also called **EW**. The three major subdivisions within electronic warfare are: electronic attack, electronic protection, and electronic warfare support. a. **electronic attack**. That division of electronic warfare involving the use of electromagnetic energy, directed energy, or antiradiation weapons to attack personnel, facilities, or equipment with the intent of degrading, neutralizing, or destroying enemy combat capability and is considered a form of fires. Also called **EA**. EA includes: 1) actions taken to prevent or reduce an enemy's effective use of the electromagnetic spectrum, such as jamming and electromagnetic deception, and 2) employment of weapons that use either electromagnetic or directed energy as their primary destructive mechanism (lasers, radio frequency weapons, particle beams). b. **electronic protection**. That division of electronic warfare involving passive and active means taken to protect personnel, facilities, and equipment from any effects of friendly or enemy employment of electronic warfare that degrade, neutralize, or destroy friendly combat capability. Also called **EP**. c. **electronic warfare support**. That division of electronic warfare involving actions tasked by, or under direct control of, an operational commander to search for, intercept, identify, and locate or localize sources of intentional and unintentional radiated electromagnetic energy for the purpose of immediate threat recognition, targeting, planning, and conduct of future operations. Thus, electronic warfare support provides information required for decisions involving electronic warfare operations and other tactical actions such as threat avoidance, targeting, and homing. Also called **ES**. Electronic warfare support data can be used to produce signals intelligence, provide targeting for electronic or destructive attack, and produce measurement and signature intelligence. (JP 1-02)

electronic warfare operations. The integrated planning, employment, and assessment of military capabilities to achieve desired effects across the electromagnetic domain in support of operational objectives. Also called **EW Ops**. (AFDD 2-5)

Global Information Grid. The globally interconnected, end-to-end set of information capabilities, associated processes and personnel for collecting, processing, storing, disseminating, and managing information on demand to warfighters, policy makers, and support personnel. The Global Information Grid (GIG) includes all owned and leased communications and computing systems and services, software (including applications), data, security services, and other associated services necessary to achieve information superiority. It also includes National Security Systems as defined in section 5142 of the Clinger-Cohen Act of 1996. The

GIG supports all Department of Defense (DOD), National Security, and related intelligence community missions and functions (strategic, operational, tactical, and business), in war and in peace. The GIG provides capabilities from all operating locations (bases, posts, camps, stations, facilities, mobile platforms, and deployed sites). The GIG provides interfaces to coalition, allied, and non-DOD users and systems. Also called **GIG.** (JP 1-02)

influence operations. Employment of capabilities to affect behaviors, protect operations, communicate commander's intent, and project accurate information to achieve desired effects across the cognitive domain. These effects should result in differing behavior or a change in the adversary decision cycle, which aligns with the commander's objectives (AFDD 2-5)

information. 1. Facts, data, or instructions in any medium or form. 2. The meaning that a human assigns to data by means of the known conventions used in their representation. (JP 1-02)

information assurance. Information operations that protect and defend information and information systems by ensuring their availability, integrity, authentication, confidentiality, and non-repudiation. This includes providing for restoration of information systems by incorporating protection, detection, and reaction capabilities. Also called **IA.** See also information; information operations; information system. (JP 1-02) [The Air Force prefers the DOD definition found in DODD 8500.1 *"Measures that protect and defend information and information systems by ensuring their availability, integrity, authentication, confidentiality, and nonrepudiation. This includes providing for restoration of information systems by incorporating protection, detection, and reaction capabilities"*]

information dissemination management. The subset of information management with a supporting infrastructure that addresses awareness, access, and delivery of information. The primary mission is to provide the right information to the right person, in the right format, at the right place and time in accordance with commanders' information dissemination policies while optimizing the use of information infrastructure resources. It involves the compilation, cataloging, caching, distribution, and retrieval of data; manages the information flow to users; and enables the execution of the commanders' information dissemination policy. (AFDD 2-5)

information environment. The aggregate of individuals, organizations, or systems that collect, process, or disseminate information; also included is the information itself. (JP 1-02)

information operations. Actions taken to affect adversary information and information systems while defending one's own information and information systems. Also called **IO.** (JP 1-02) [*Information operations are the integrated employment of the core capabilities of influence operations, electronic warfare operations, network warfare operations, in concert with specified integrated control enablers, to influence, disrupt, corrupt or usurp adversarial human and automated decision making while protecting our own.*] (AFDD 2-5) {Italicized definition in brackets applies only to the Air Force and is offered for clarity.}

information superiority. That degree of dominance in the information domain which permits the conduct of operations without effective opposition. (JP 1-02) The Air Force prefers to cast 'superiority' as a state of relative advantage, not a capability, and views information superiority as: [*the degree of dominance in the information domain which allows friendly forces the ability to collect, control, exploit, and defend information without effective opposition.*] (AFDD 2-5) {Italicized definition in brackets applies only to the Air Force and is offered for clarity.}

information system. The entire infrastructure, organization, personnel, and components that collect, process, store, transmit, display, disseminate, and act on information. (JP 1-02)

information technology. An umbrella term describing the suite of tools used for managing and processing information. These tools can include any communications device or computer, its ancillary equipment, software applications, and related supporting resources. Also called **IT**. (AFDD 2-5)

information warfare. Information operations conducted during time of crisis or conflict to achieve or promote specific objectives over a specific adversary or adversaries. Also called **IW**. (JP 1-02) [*The theory of warfare in the information environment that guides the application of information operations to produce specific battlespace effect in support of commander's objectives.*] (AFDD 2-5) {Italicized definition in brackets applies only to the Air Force and is offered for clarity.}

integrated control enablers. Critical capabilities required to execute successful air, space, and information operations and produce integrated effects for the joint fight. Includes intelligence, surveillance, and reconnaissance, network operations, and precision navigation and timing. Also called **ICE**. (AFDD 2-5)

intelligence. 1. The product resulting from the collection, processing, integration, analysis, evaluation, and interpretation of available information concerning foreign countries or areas. 2. Information and knowledge about an adversary obtained through observation, investigation, analysis, or understanding. (JP 1-02)

intelligence preparation of the battlespace. An analytical methodology employed to reduce uncertainties concerning the enemy, environment, and terrain for all types of operations. Intelligence preparation of the battlespace builds an extensive database for each potential area in which a unit may be required to operate. The database is then analyzed in detail to determine the impact of the enemy, environment, and terrain on operations and presents it in graphic form. Intelligence preparation of the battlespace is a continuing process. Also called **IPB**. (JP 1-02)

intelligence, surveillance, and reconnaissance. Intelligence, surveillance, and reconnaissance are integrated capabilities to collect, process, exploit, and disseminate accurate and timely information that provides the battlespace awareness necessary to successfully plan and conduct operations. Also called **ISR**. (AFDD 2-9)

military deception. Actions executed to deliberately mislead adversary military decision makers as to friendly military capabilities, intentions, and operations, thereby causing the adversary to take specific actions (or inactions) that will contribute to the accomplishment of the friendly mission. (JP 1-02) [There are five categories of military deception. See JP 1-02 for complete definition.]

network attack. The employment of network-based capabilities to destroy, disrupt, corrupt, or usurp information resident in or transiting through networks. Networks include telephony and data services networks. Also called **NetA.** (AFDD 2-5)

network defense. The employment of network-based capabilities to defend friendly information resident in or transiting through networks against adversary efforts to destroy, disrupt, corrupt, or usurp it. Also called **NetD.** (AFDD 2-5)

network management. The execution of the set of activities required for controlling, planning, allocating, deploying, coordinating, and monitoring the resources of a telecommunications network, including performing actions such as initial network planning, frequency allocation, predetermined traffic routing to support load balancing, cryptographic key distribution authorization, configuration management, fault management, security management, performance management, and accounting management. (AFDD 2-5)

network operations (NetOps). The integrated planning and employment of military capabilities to provide the friendly net environment needed to plan, control and execute military operations and conduct Service functions. NetOps provides operational planning and control. It involves time-critical, operational-level decisions that direct configuration changes and information routing. NetOps risk management and command and control decisions are based on a fused assessment of intelligence, ongoing operations, commander's intent, blue and gray situation, net health, and net security. NetOps provides the three operational elements of information assurance, network/system management, and information dissemination management. Also called **NetOps.**

network warfare operations. Network warfare operations are the integrated planning and employment of military capabilities to achieve desired effects across the interconnected analog and digital portion of the battlespace. Network warfare operations are conducted in the information domain through the dynamic combination of hardware, software, data, and human interaction. Also called **NW Ops.** (AFDD 2-5)

network warfare support. Actions tasked by or under direct control of an operational commander to search for, intercept, identify, and locate or localize sources of access and vulnerability for the purpose of immediate threat recognition, targeting, planning, and conduct of future operations. NS provides information required for immediate decisions involving network warfare operations. NS data can be used to produce intelligence, or provide targeting for electronic or destructive attack. Also called **NS.** (AFDD 2-5)

OODA loop. A theory developed by Col. John Boyd (USAF, Ret.) contending that one can depict all rational human behavior, individual and organizational, as a continual cycling through four distinct tasks: observation, orientation, decision, and action. (AFDD 2-5)

operations security. A process of identifying critical information and subsequently analyzing friendly actions attendant to military operations and other activities to: a. identify those actions that can be observed by adversary intelligence systems; b. determine indicators that hostile intelligence systems might obtain that could be interpreted or pieced together to derive critical information in time to be useful to adversaries; and c. select and execute measures that eliminate or reduce to an acceptable level the vulnerabilities of friendly actions to adversary exploitation. Also called **OPSEC**. (JP 1-02)

psychological operations. Planned operations to convey selected information and indicators to foreign audiences to influence their emotions, motives, objective reasoning, and ultimately the behavior of foreign governments, organizations, groups, and individuals. The purpose of psychological operations is to induce or reinforce foreign attitudes and behavior favorable to the originator's objectives. Also called **PSYOP**. (JP 1-02)

tactical digital information link. A Joint Staff-approved, standardized communication link suitable for transmission of digital information. Tactical digital information links interface two or more command and control or weapons systems via a single or multiple network architecture and multiple communication media for exchange of tactical information. Also called **TADIL**. (JP 1-02)